The Ultimate
College
PRANK BOOK

DISCLAIMER: We are not responsible for any suc[...] may experience in your college career as a result of this book, either socially, politically, romantical[...] he[...]wise. We take no responsibility whatsoever for your future aspirations, your relationship with [...] b[...]ngs, your professors, or your friends. We don't care, nor do we feel bad about the fact that yo[...]ng [...]ed[...]ral priso[...] Some, if not all, of the ideas presented in this book are dangerous and potentiall[...] and are a[...]oar[...]ying to someone, so don't say you haven't been warned.

Mae B. Expelled

adamsmedia

Avon, Massachusetts

Published by
Adams Media, a division of F+W Media, Inc.
57 Littlefield Street, Avon, MA 02322. U.S.A.
www.adamsmedia.com

ISBN 10: 1-4405-0340-0
ISBN 13: 978-1-4405-0340-5

Printed in the United States of America.

J I H G F E D C B A

Library of Congress Cataloging-in-Publication Data
is available from the publisher.

This publication is designed to provide accurate and authoritative information with regard to the subject matter covered. It is sold with the understanding that the publisher is not engaged in rendering legal, accounting, or other professional advice. If legal advice or other expert assistance is required, the services of a competent professional person should be sought.
　　　　—From a *Declaration of Principles* jointly adopted by a Committee of the American Bar Association and a Committee of Publishers and Associations

Many of the designations used by manufacturers and sellers to distinguish their product are claimed as trademarks. Where those designations appear in this book and Adams Media was aware of a trademark claim, the designations have been printed with initial capital letters.

Due to the potential for hazard, every precaution should be taken before attempting any actions listed in this book. The author, Adams Media, and F+W Media, Inc. do not accept liability for any injury, loss, or incidental or consequential damage incurred by reliance on the information or advice provided in this book.

Interior illustrations by Elisabeth Lariviere
Pushpin by Elisabeth Lariviere

This book is available at quantity discounts for bulk purchases.
For information, please call 1-800-289-0963.

Contents

DISCLAIMER:

Mae B. Expelled and the Publisher would like you to know that we are not responsible for any success or failure you may experience in your college career as a result of this book either socially, politically, romantically, academically, or otherwise. We take no responsibility whatsoever for your future aspirations, your relationship with your parents, your siblings, your professors, or your friends. We don't care, nor do we feel bad about the fact that you are serving time in a federal prison. We aren't interested in your sob story about the letter you got that was not a prank (even though it looked similar to the letterhead you yourself forged) expressing that "You are not, nor ever shall you be invited back to The University of Pull Your Head Out of Your Ass." And we really don't think it's any of our concern that you got banned from Spring Fling, the school theater, two of six cafeterias, or English class. Some, if not all of the ideas presented in this book are dangerous and potentially fatal and are across the board annoying to someone, so don't say you haven't been warned. Also, since you are now eighteen, we'd like to remind you that your parents will not be standing trial on your behalf and you will not be tried as a minor no matter how immature you are.

We repeat: Some of these pranks will certainly get you expelled and some will get you into serious legal trouble. Others are just plain dangerous. And a few are really gross. So engage in these antics at your own risk.

Welcome to Hellshire University

Where Hades teaches Intro to Purgatory and the Devil is the dean.

Your college years are made up of a whole lot of identity seeking and, inevitably, a whole lot of identity seekers. For example, that douche in your Women's Studies class, **Will Do Anything to Get Some**, just dropped a pencil to look up the hot chick's skirt. Meanwhile, **Always Raises Her Hand** may as well take off her shirt, she's so eager for the professor (and everybody else) to like her. **Smokes His Breakfast**'s head just landed on your shoulder when he passed out. Your roommate, **Never Drinks Water**, is calling your cell to ask you if you ashed in the orphaned beer on the kitchen table or if it is safe to drink. And saddest of all, your huge crush has earned the nickname **Fire Crotch**.

There you are, in the middle of it all, trying to make some sense out of why in God's name you made the decision to skip the post–high school European backpacking trip or the internship at *Vogue* to spend four years in this hellhole full of Greeks, divas, tweekers, and jocks. It's just high school except higher. May as well give them something to really laugh at. After all, they didn't invent photography classes just to develop photos of landscapes. How much funnier would it be if the image that appeared in the solution was that of **Professor Gasbag** canoodling with his mistress, **Alterna-Chick**, who mans the darkroom during the late shift?

All the pranks are neatly divided into sections, so you know whether or not you'll need running shoes, a get-away car, or a ticket to Mexico. If you go too far, you might be in for **A Talkin' To** by your RA, supervisor, or perhaps even a dean, so be sure to Cover Your Ass (CYA)! But if you go even farther don't say you haven't been warned that **Expulsion** or even **Incarceration** could be on your horizon. Not that you need to worry. After all, you are young and probably called **Limited Foresight** in some circles. You can start with **Freshman** jokes that are as innocent as a whoopee cushion in a Sorority House. If you are already one year in, and plain-old bored, go ahead and start with the more ambitious **Sophomore** pranks. **Junior-** and **Senior**-level stunts will really shock and terrify the **Do-Gooding Hippie** and give the **TA with the `Tude** a little attitude adjustment. Finally, show the **Creepy and Antisocial** bunch that there's more to life than video games and the library.

Go ahead. You've been dared. Now it's your turn to put the "under" in "undergraduate. . . ."

University Directory

There's no need to spend a lot of time and money gathering basic information like names, numbers, e-mail addresses, and the general housing and office locations of your prank targets. After all, your school has already done it for you. The university directory is the prankster's most valuable resource. Keep it close, like your enemies.

Name: Alterna-Chick
Phone: THE-CURE
E-mail: blackbutterfly@hellshire.edu
Address: Morrissey Hall
Most likely to: Wear baby doll dresses with combat boots and get her nose pierced as soon as her parents drive away from campus

Name: Always Raises Her Hand
Phone: 444-4444
E-mail: Hermione_Granger@hellshire.edu
Address: Her parents' house
Most likely to: Moan a little when she raises her hand

Name: Anal RA
Phone: 444-STOP
E-mail: Ididitallwhenlwasyourage@hellshire.edu
Address: Up your ass
Most likely to: Watch your every move

Name: Backwards Baseball Cap
Phone: 1-800-CALL-BABE
E-mail: sayheykid@hellshire.edu
Address: The jock dorm
Most likely to: Dip and spit

Name: Creepy and Antisocial
Phone: Unlisted
E-mail: trenchcoatwearer@hellshire.edu
Address: An unused broom closet at the back of the old gym (at least, that's where his gun collection lives and therefore, where he spends most of his time)
Most likely to: Blow something up

Name: Divorced Old Guy
Phone: TOM-JONE(S)
E-mail: disco-lives@hellshire.edu
Address: Bachelor pad off campus
Most likely to: Date a different hot freshman every term

Name: Do-Gooding Hippie
Phone: SUN-LOVE
E-mail: HeartsTrees@hellshire.edu
Address: The E House
Most likely to: Wear tie-dye, have a shrine to Jerry Garcia, and
dance with her eyes closed

Name: Euro-Trash
Phone: LEA-THER
E-mail: openshirt_hairychest@hellshire.edu
Address: A downtown nightclub—at least he smells like he
lives there
Most likely to: Create an oil slick when his hair melts

Name: Fire Crotch
Phone: LEG-OPEN
E-mail: nopanties@hellshire.edu
Address: Her current boyfriend's house
Most likely to: Give scabies to the dean of admissions, the dean
of students, and the president of the university in that order

Name: Graveyard Goth
Phone: 666-6666
E-mail: bloodykittens@hellshire.edu
Address: The Marilyn Manson Commons
Most likely to: Conduct readings of *Helter Skelter* in graveyards

Name: Greek Asshole
Phone: KAPP-PSI
E-mail: can_smasher@hellshire.edu
Address: Delta Kappa Psi House
Most likely to: Paddle the bare asses of prospective freshmen
(and like it)

Name: Limited Foresight
Phone: 911
E-mail: alwaysinjured@hellshire.edu
Address: County General
Most likely to: Climb the town water tower and fall off due to poor
planning

Name: Never Drinks Water
Phone: 444-BEER
E-mail: onedollarpabstnight@hellshire.edu
Address: Busch Hall
Most likely to: Be hospitalized due to alcohol poisoning

Name: Only Speaks Football
Phone: GOO-TEAM
E-mail: rosebowlbound@hellshire.edu
Address: The Dog Pound or the Wildcat Den
Most likely to: Choke on a hotdog while screaming at the ref, the
coach, or the players that even his grandma coulda' scored that
fucking goal!

Name: Pasty Library Geek
Phone: WHO-LUV-MATH
E-mail: from_einstein_to_dickinson@hellshire.edu
Address: The Library Stacks
Most likely to: Die of a severe vitamin D deficiency and have the
periodic table of elements memorized

Name: Smokes His Breakfast
Phone: Huh?
E-mail: Dude . . .
Address: Wait. What was the question?
Most likely to: Master the art of creating pipes out of aluminum cans, fruit, and ice cubes

Name: Sorority Spirit
Phone: AIR-HEAD
E-mail: deltadeltadeltamayihelpyahelpyahelpya@hellshire.edu
Address: The Tri Delt House
Most likely to: Lock herself in her car

Name: Will Do Anything to Get Some
Phone: What's *your* phone number?
E-mail: howYOUdoin@hellshire.edu
Address: Whatever you want it to be
Most likely to: Do the Naked Quad Run to see if he can "accidentally" bump into girls

Faculty Directory

Name: President PompASS
Phone: Unavailable
E-mail: E-mail his secretary
Office location: None of your business
Office hours: Yeah right

Name: Professor Buttons Unbuttoned
Phone: 1-HOT-FOR-PROF
E-mail: only_a_few_years_older_than_her_students@hellshire.edu
Office location: French Department
Office hours: 10:15 P.M.–Midnight, Fridays and Saturdays

Name: Professor Gasbag
Phone: 444-TALK
E-mail: Iknoweverything@hellshire.edu
Office location: Music, Photography, English, Math, and History Departments
Office hours: Whenever he is not working on his book

Name: TA with the 'Tude
Phone: TOO-BUSY
E-mail: rollinghiseyes@hellshire.edu
Office location: His family housing apartment
Office hours: 4–6 P.M., Mon., Wed., and Fri. (if the baby isn't sick while his wife is at work—actually, just e-mail him)

Entrance Exam

Answer the following questions to determine the kind of accomplice you need to seek out, if any, for any prank you pull.

Choosing an accomplice is serious business. You are residing in a virtual cesspool of bored, horny, and excitable teenagers, all of whom are in the prime of their moral ambiguity and most of whom enjoy a fearlessness that borders on stupidity. The more accomplices you enlist, the harder it becomes to keep everyone quiet and straight-faced. So, pick them carefully and specifically. In the event that you find yourself debating between a person with mad tech skills and one with a back like a bull, answer the following questions about the prank you intend to pull to figure out who will come in the handiest. Use the best answer even if more than one answer applies.

1. This prank requires that the target . . .

a. Believe he or she is being contacted by a professional organization
b. Be confused by a new or altered structure
c. Fall for someone
d. Join a group

2. The target of your prank is expected to . . .

a. Be afraid
b. Get wet or dirty
c. Be embarrassed
d. Start a fight

3. The ideal accomplice for this prank will have . . .

a. Great computer skills
b. Big biceps
c. Short skirts or tight jeans
d. The ability to make a lot of noise

4. You really could use someone who works . . .

a. In the computer lab
b. With the janitorial staff
c. Out
d. Quickly

5. The prank must be completed . . .

a. Any time of the day or night with a lot of time to get it together
b. Overnight
c. In the evening, preferably by candle light
d. During normal waking hours

6. For the prank to work, the target must live . . .

a. With a computer, a cell phone, and/or campus mail
b. In a dormitory
c. In a same-sex residence
d. It doesn't matter

7. Your accomplice must be comfortable . . .

a. Performing white-collar crimes
b. Picking locks and hotwiring cars
c. Wearing a push-up bra
d. Pretending like everything is normal

8. The goal of your prank is to . . .

a. Get something from the target
b. Confuse or soil the target
c. Humiliate the target
d. Teach the target a lesson

Congratulations. You have finished the test. Reward yourself with a shot of tequila, wheat germ, or bong water, depending on your mood. Then move on to the results. You won't need a calculator, just two hands. Count your A's, your B's, your C's, and your D's.

Did you answer mostly A's?

You require a serious tech geek to help you pull off this prank. Chances are you are looking to rewire something, break down firewalls, or create important-looking paraphernalia. All of these are best served by a person who spoke computer before he spoke the ABC's.

Did you answer mostly B's?

You probably need someone to do some heavy lifting and other tasks requiring physical labor. This accomplice need not be the sharpest knife in the drawer; in fact, dumber might be better, but it would help if this person is accomplished at scaling fences, climbing trees, and breaking into things.

Did you answer mostly C's?

This prank requires that you find an accomplice with a tight ass and a shake in the walk. You need your target to *care*, which is best accomplished through a denial of food, water, or love. Since the first two are a surefire way to find yourself incarcerated, the third is your best bet. So find a hottie. The Drama Department might be a great place to look. Because a hottie who can *act* is the most valuable accomplice in all of prankdom.

Did you answer mostly D's?

This prank seems like it will come off the best if you enlist the help of a group. Using friends is obviously easiest. However, you can lure the aged and the young by posting on craigslist or creating a campus club. Might even be a hilarious prank to start a bird-watching club that serves as a beard for the Merry Band of Pranksters Club it actually is.

Freshman Pranks

Pranks for the Young, Innocent, and Generally Confused

If you are still using a map to find your way to Intro to Basic English and traveling in a pack of six or more either metaphorically or literally, these are the pranks for you. They are unlikely to get you into the kind of trouble that requires a parent who works as an international diplomat, nor are they going to make you many friends, but they should arm you with the kind of story that will lead to someone at the table snorting milk out of his nose as it is relayed over breakfast.

In Your Face

TARGET: Never Drinks Water

Tools

Five to ten cans of shaving cream (depending on desired fluffiness of pillow), a pillow case

You've finally had it when for the third time this week your roommate **Never Drinks Water** mistakes your laundry basket for the urinal. As he begins reaching for his tenth lager, you are pretty sure you know what will happen next. He'll get halfway through it and his head will fall—where? That's right, straight onto his pillow. What he doesn't know is that you have swapped his fancy Tempur-Pedic stuffing for about five cans of fluffy shaving cream. The best part will be when he falls over. The second best part will be when he wakes up in the morning with a face full of foam.

CYA

Tell him you saw a couple of thugs from the hockey team running out of the room when you came back from your evening shower. That's all you know and you're sticking to it.

Greek Tragedy

TARGET: Greek Asshole

Mention to someone that you heard that the fraternities are being shut down due to excessive alcohol consumption. The power of a simple word-of-mouth rumor cannot be underestimated. Universities have been spreading this rumor for years to get fraternities to cut back on their drinking, and for some reason people never stop falling for it.

If the word doesn't spread organically, try sending a formal-looking letter to the school paper with an anonymous note on fraternity letterhead promising a good fight with the National Panhellenic Conference and the North-American Interfraternity Conference if they don't repeal their "decision."

Prank Pitfall

The frat houses might dry out for a little while in order to fly the straight and narrow until the winds change. And that's where everybody loses, my friend.

Chalkboard Admirer

TARGET: Always Raises Her Hand

Every day write a new message on the chalkboard as if you are **Always Raises Her Hand**'s secret admirer. Be sneaky. And creative. Try messages like, "My heart is so full of love for a woman who knows the answer to every question, especially the answer to the question of my heart."

CYA

Have a different person leave the message each day before class and change up the handwriting to throw her off the scent. If she catches you in the act, tell her that someone in a black cap paid you $25 to write the message and that's all you know.

♡ My heart aches for the woman who knows the answer to every question...

Prank Pitfall

She might decide you're hot.

E-Mail Attack

TARGET: Divorced Old Guy

You have 27 New e-mails!

Get as many people as you can to e-mail your target the same e-mail: "Ashley told me you have a crush on me." "Ashley" can be changed to any other name. **Divorced Old Guy** will not know where to begin to deny the rumors and will likely spend his time looking for someone named Ashley who it turns out doesn't exist.

Fingers and Toes

TARGET: Greek Asshole

Tools *Nail polish or a colored marker*

Once your man passes out after a big night of tail-chasing and misogyny, give that closeted boy a little color on his hands and feet. Simply paint his nails. That's enough to wake him up red-faced and horrified as he calls the fraternity sweetheart to see if he can borrow her nail polish remover. What could be funnier?

Angel Dust

TARGET: Fire Crotch

Sisters

Tools

White inexpensive powder, a hair dryer

Fire Crotch is getting ready for another date. She is currently in the shower. Grab her hair dryer and fill it with a good clump of talcum powder (flour, baby powder, baking powder, or cornstarch can substitute). Hide in a toilet stall and come out just moments before she begins drying her shiny clean locks. Catch her reaction when she turns on the hair dryer and catches a mouthful, earful, or head-full of the fabulous white powder.

Till the Cows Come Home

TARGET: Cafeteria staff

Tools

Phone (preferably untraceable!)

Call the school cafeteria and tell them you have a cow you'd like to sell them for $100. When they ask where you are, tell them you are on campus. If they press you, tell them you are in the dorm. When they repeat for clarification, "You are in the dorm with a cow?" answer simply, "Yes. And I want to sell it." Make sure you mention that it produces about a gallon of milk per day, is very good with children, and has put on quite a bit of weight since you found her in the gymnasium last September. The key here is total deadpan honesty no matter what question they throw at you.

Questions you should be prepared to answer:

- Where'd you get it?
- How much does it weigh?
- Does the school know? and
- Can we get it for $80?

Weeping Willows

TARGET: Everyone

Accomplices: As many as you can find

Tools

Copious amounts of toilet paper, preferably stolen from various dormitories and academic halls

This is exactly the same as the time that you t.p.'d Laura McGillicutty's house for calling you a slut in sixth grade except on a grander scheme (and with less venom). Cover as many trees as possible in cascading white tumbling rolls. It will look beautiful under a full moon. Even better if you can shine black lights on your creation.

CYA

*Call it art and blame your art teacher for freeing the creative genius inside of you. Reference **The Gates at Central Park** by Christo and Jeanne-Claude. They got paid millions for that eyesore! At least yours will break down easily after the next rain.*

Scene of the Crime

TARGET: Only Speaks Football

Tools

Chalk, ketchup, police tape

One night, after the big game, lead **Only Speaks Football** on a walk he doesn't usually take. Tell him you are so amped up, you just want to "walk it off." Somewhere in a quiet corner of campus, happen upon the chalk outline of two or three bodies. What **Only Speaks Football** does not know is that you drew them earlier in the night. Try to make the crime scene look like it has been cleaned up with a few broken pieces of police tape and maybe even a little bit of dried ketchup. See if your target doesn't suddenly have more to talk about than a missed goal or the cheerleader with the split seam.

Missing Underpants

TARGET: Pasty Library Geek

Your study partner, **Pasty Library Geek**, is in her regular cubicle at the library. One day when you are feeling bored and *don't* feel like studying, see if you can get her roommate to let you in to switch her drawers around. Put her underpants where her shirts usually are and move her pants down to her sock drawer. Once everything is scrambled, the next time she comes home it will be hysterical to watch her unscramble it.

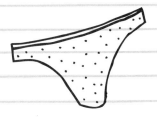

Prank Pitfall

She won't be going back to the library until she sorts all her clothes out, which isn't funny if you need her to help you cram for the Anthro exam.

Let the Music Play

TARGET: Euro-Trash

Tools

A record sleeve and a can of shaving cream

In this simple prank, fill the empty sleeve of an old LP with shaving cream. It can easily be slipped under most doors. Face the open end into the room. When Euro gets up with the grease from his hair in his eyes, he'll unknowingly step on it and spray shaving cream all over his room.

Push Your Luck: Place record sleeves full of shaving cream all over the room while your target is sleeping. When he gets out of bed, watch the shaving cream fly!

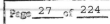

The Pickup Artist

TARGET: Alterna-Chick

Accomplices: Two believable friends

Approach **Alterna-Chick** in the cafeteria or library and pick her up doing your best Rico Suave. Try to get her to give you her address or number. While you are there, have two of your friends posing as "counselors" approach. Make sure you look disappointed or annoyed. Have one of them say, "Let's go," to you and lead you away. The other should stay and explain to the girl that you are a patient at a nearby mental health facility who is one of the first to try a new outpatient program where you are supposed to be under the surveillance of a counselor at all times while taking college classes. Have the accomplice ask her if you tried to get money or drugs from her. Then have them apologize for taking her time and warn her to watch out for you.

Presidential Mail

TARGET: President PompASS

Tools
E-mail, telephone

The goal here is to generate as much paper mail as possible. Using a fake e-mail, write to various travel agencies asking for brochures about cities **President PompASS** is planning on traveling to. You can also call claiming to be his wife. Just tell them to send any information they have to your husband's office. You can also call for catalogs and further information on furniture or timeshares.

Push Your Luck: Publish an article in the school paper about the wasteful paper mail the university creates. Point specifically to the **President's** overflowing mailbox. Not only should the school make sure he is recycling, but he needs to be sure to make a point of giving something back to mother Earth.

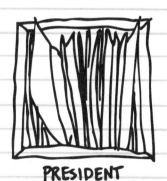

PRESIDENT
POMPASS

Coo-Coo Clock

TARGET: Euro-Trash
Accomplice: Euro's roommate

So, your neighbor **Euro-Trash** got in late again from the clubs. For the third time this week he is liberally slapping the snooze button on his alarm clock. His slapping is in fact so vigorous, you are ready to slap him up side the head. It's time to teach this greaseball a lesson.

Record the sound of the alarm clock as perfectly as possible. (Alternative option, buy an identical clock.) Using his roommate as your accomplice, hide the recording near Euro-Trash's clock. Set off the fake alarm and watch as the snoozing slickster slaps wildly at the button.

Inevitably he will unplug it in his vain attempt to find silence. When his head explodes, your mission is accomplished.

If that doesn't teach him a lesson, hide the keys to his Vespa.

Witches Brew

TARGET: Graveyard Goth

Tools

Dry ice and Tupperware

Dry ice is just plain fun. Put some in a piece of Tupperware that floats in the toilet bowl. Too much dry ice will sink the Tupperware, but a small amount will work, and the Tupperware will continue to float above the water. Now, when **Goth** pees into the bowl, she will be amazed when her urine starts to smoke! But that's what happens when liquid lands on dry ice—steam, smoky steam! Fantastic.

Prank Pitfall

If your target looks into the toilet before peeing, she'll probably switch to a different stall.

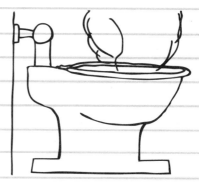

Poop Pool

TARGET: Backwards Baseball Cap

Tools
Baby Ruth candy bar

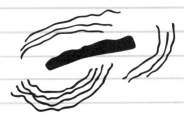

We've all heard this one, but for your buddy **Baseball Cap**, who is on the swim team, it's a funny one. Simply throw a Baby Ruth candy bar into the pool where your target can't miss it. Then walk away. Let the candy bar do the rest. Since you know what it looks like as it floats along, you can imagine what "the rest" is.

Push Your Luck: Go a second time and drop a Baby Ruth into the pool. You are likely to get a similar reaction. Then, on your third time, put an actual poop, human or canine, into the pool. When **Baseball Cap** calmly tells everyone, "Don't worry! It's just a Baby Ruth" and pulls it out, he'll be in for a (not-so-sweet) surprise.

Prank Pitfall
There is probably some law against putting actual crap in the pool. I am not a lawyer, so I have no idea. Also, the pool will have to be drained and cleaned. So if you're also a swimmer, you will not be able to swim until the pool has been cleaned and disinfected.

Sun-Stained

TARGET: Will Do Anything to Get Some

Tools

The kind of shaving cream that dispenses as gel and turns into foam when meeting the air

The thing about this particular kind of gel shaving cream is that it bakes in the sun on black top and turns a surprising shade of glistening gold. Also, it doesn't wash off. In fact, there are documented cases of driveways requiring repaving in order to get it off.

To ensure that your message will stand the test of time, choose a sunny weekend when that loser **Will Do Anything** is going to be out for a while. One Friday night, dress in black and leave him a message in bold block letters. It can be friendly:

"You Rock in the Sack!" or not so friendly, "Too bad you're so ugly." Then leave Mother Nature to dry the message into something long lasting and gold.

Prank Pitfall

Did I mention that it doesn't wash off? As in, repaving is the only solution here? You have been warned. Now go graffiti.

Tardy Test Taker

TARGET: Pasty Library Geek

This is a pretty straight-forward prank and can be used for everything from exams to events. In this case, after **Pasty Library Geek** falls asleep the night before a big exam, set all the clocks in the apartment ahead by two hours, then set her clock alarm ahead by one hour from the time at which she had it set. When she wakes up, she will think she's late, wildly get dressed and run out the door. By the time she checks her cell phone and figures out what has happened, it will be almost time for her exam, so chances are she'll go get a coffee and deal with you later.

CYA

Deny, deny, deny.

Penny Pusher

TARGET: Creepy and Antisocial

Tools

Pennies and a hammer

When **Creepy** closes his door for the night, make sure he can't get back out. If you are outside looking at the door, on the left side is the handle and the right side is the hinge. If you jam pennies into the right-side crack, the door will not open and **Creepy** will be stuck inside. He deserves it because he's probably drowning rodents in that stinking cave from which he so rarely emerges.

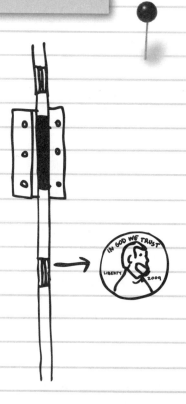

Prank Pitfall

He might hunt you down and shoot your ass.

The Puke Special

TARGET: Never Drinks Water

Tools

A funnel, a pint carton of milk, and a pint carton of OJ

One night after another hard day of drinking, surprise your hungover target with this excellent prank.

Begin by emptying a pint carton of milk into a pitcher. Then put the funnel into the mouth of the carton and pour in the contents of the pint carton of OJ. You see where this is going. Last step? Pour the milk into the OJ carton. The next day when **Never** pours himself a cup of coffee and adds the milk, won't he be surprised! Even better is if he goes for a bowl of Sugar Smacks and ends up with a sweetened orange-y disaster. This prank guarantees a full-on puke fest, so follow your boy with a bucket.

Prank Pitfall

Careful you don't forget that you did this or you could pay the price of the prank! Also, watch out for innocent bystanders.

Double Dating

TARGET: Anal RA

<u>Tools</u>

An anonymous computer

Set up a fake dating pro-
file for your RA. This is
especially satisfying if
he is already in a rela-
tionship. Then make him
an active player online,
sending notes containing
his e-mail to as many people as possible, both men
and women—because making
gay people straight and
straight people gay is automatically funny.

CYA

*Make sure you cover all
your steps. Use a public
computer. Deny involve-
ment or you risk being
accused of smoking pot
through dryer sheets
without a shred of evi-
dence. He can do that.
He's the RA.*

Ransom

TARGET: Always Raises Her Hand

Tools

A fake e-mail address

Always is a good target for this prank because you *know* she has a stuffed animal in her room. Kidnap the animal. Now, take pictures of the animal in various places, perhaps even performing "unsavory acts." E-mail the pictures to **Always** as if you are a kidnapper. Use a fake e-mail account. Let her know that Snuffles will remain alive as long as she complies with the terms of ransom. These can be whatever you want: a sum of money, a baked good, help with a paper.

You could also steal someone's favorite T-shirt, a meaningful lighter, wallet, purse, or other object of value (financial or personal) and carry out the same prank. But Snuffles is funnier.

Prank Pitfall

If you do try to get money out of your target, you are risking criminal behavior. Sticking to baked goods as ransom is less likely to get you into serious trouble and keeps things light and funny.

Dead Line

TARGET: Professor Buttons Unbuttoned

Sneak into **Buttons Unbuttoned**'s office and tape the receiver button down on the telephone. This is an oldie but a goodie if your school still has phones with receiver buttons and not the newfangled cordless kinds.

Prank Pitfall

In the event that you get caught sneaking into your professor's office when she is not there, you will ask yourself if the potential four seconds of glory was worth it.

Abe Lincoln's Breath

TARGET: Old Divorced Guy

Tools
A Ziploc baggie

Give **Old Divorced Guy** a present. Strike up a conversation about our nation's sixteenth president with him. A few days later tell him you got him something on eBay based on your debate from the other day. Meanwhile, mail a box to him containing a sealed plastic baggie with the writing, "Abraham Lincoln's Last Breath, April 15, 1865, 7:22 A.M." Little does he know, you have filled that baggie with several of your best bean-eating farts.

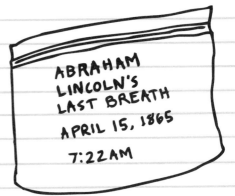

Breakfast at Tiffany's

TARGET: Fire Crotch

<u>Tools</u>

A blue Tiffany's gift box

Send the lovely Miss **Crotch** a fabulous gift that will really get her heart racing. These little blue boxes signify something truly spectacular to come. Make sure you give it to her on her birthday or for a holiday so she isn't suspicious. Then tell her it's no big deal. Your dad works in real estate and rents to one of the Tiffany's branches in Vegas. She'll be used to getting nice gifts from male admirers. Watch her fingers shake as she opens it up. Then watch the color drain out of her face when she sees the simple words

"Happy Birthday Sucker!" on an index card inside.

Tiffany bracelet: $2,500. Look on **Fire Crotch**'s face when she discovers the index card? Priceless.

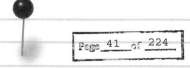

Bug Juice

TARGET: Greek Asshole

Tools

Those little plastic spiders, cockroaches, and flies

Are you sick of the rest of the frat brothers drinking your OJ? Using all your whole milk? Finishing the peanut butter? One way to cut down on moochers is to teach them a lesson. When you are nearing, for example, the bottom of the carton of juice, stick a plastic bug in there. The next person to pour himself a drink will be surprised by what falls out and into his glass (or more likely into his dirty little mouth if he chugs straight from the carton!).

Prank Pitfall

Those little bugs are a choking hazard. (Not that they don't deserve it.)

Hole-Punch Avalanche

TARGET: President PompASS

Tools

As many hole-punch punch-outs as you can gather, a piece of cardboard

This sounds like an office prank, but the truth is, there are few hole punchers on planet Earth more overflowing with those magical white paper circles than those found on a college campus. Go from room to room collecting them. Ideally you should not *ask* for them, you should just take them and walk out without calling attention to it. (Less chance you'll get caught.)

Now, visit the office of **President PompASS** while he is at a meeting, and put a hearty pile of the punch-outs onto the cardboard and balance it carefully on top of a slightly opened door. When the prez returns to his office, those pesky flakes will come sailing down onto his head. The goal is to make it snow!

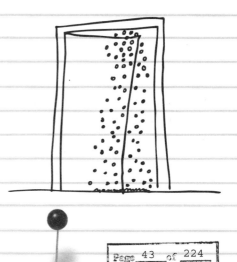

Fan Tastic

TARGET: Backwards Baseball Cap

Set up a fan page on Facebook for your boy **Backwards** through his own personal Facebook account, the password for which you must steal. (Suggestion: Watch him log in one day and pay attention to the password.) Have "him" send out invites to all of his friends to become his fans. Try to make the page look sincere. Have a list of his accomplishments including "Little League MVP 1999" and "Best Dancer at Brad's Bar Mitzvah, 2004."

facebook   Home Profile Friends Inbox

Become a fan of
Backwards Baseball Cap

Push Your Luck: Add or Photoshop pictures of **Backwards** succeeding, or in the middle of, a moment of supreme greatness—like when he won the summer camp hot dog eating contest or got the hottie to go with him to prom.

Locked Out

TARGET: Anyone who has to go to the bathroom

This is probably the easiest prank in the book and works anywhere there is an institutional restroom with stalls. Enter the stall, lock the door, and crawl out. That's it. This joke is a classic and one that is especially irritating in dirty bathrooms.

Jelly Door Handle

TARGET: Anal RA

Craig

This prank works best with the kind of handle that is enclosed and lifts up, like on most Volkswagen models. Simply stuff some jelly donut pieces under there and watch from a distance as your target opens his door and ends up with a gross handful of smeary donut!

For other kinds of handles you can smear honey or jelly along the inside for a similar, if somewhat less tactile, effect.

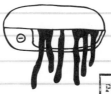

Bloody Water

TARGET: Graveyard Goth

Accomplice: Goth's roommate

Tools

Red food coloring or red drink powder

This prank comes straight out of the pages of Halloween pranks. But with **Goth** around, it's funny any time of year. For this prank, go into the kitchen cupboards and pull out all of the front-most glasses on the shelf. Sprinkle a little red drink power or red food coloring into the bottom of the glass. Chances are, she won't look before filling the glass with milk or water. If need be, help the prank along by asking **Goth** to get you a glass of water. When it pours red, she'll wonder if her last Wiccan ritual actually worked.

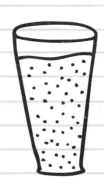

Prank Pitfall

If **Goth** is more observant than we previously realized, she might notice that the glass she is using is already dirty. In this case, choose a ditzier target, like **Sorority Spirit** next time.

Ice Bath

TARGET: Alterna-Chick

Tools
Buckets

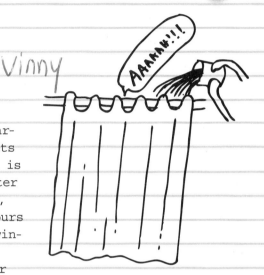

Dissed again by your tar-
get? Set up a few buckets
of cold water. The best is
if you can get your water
out of the refrigerator,
or cool it for a few hours
outside during a cold winter day. Once you are
satisfied with the water
temperature, go into the
bathroom where an unsus-
pecting **Alterna-Chick** is
taking a hot shower. Then
throw as many buckets of
cold water over the shower
curtain as you can before
she comes barreling at you
with her long, dark red
fingernails and digs them
into your face.

Prank Pitfall

You will almost definitely
get caught. So expect
payback—or the nails in
your face thing.

Inked

TARGET: Never Drinks Water
Accomplice: Someone with mad drawing skills

Tools

A Sharpie

When **Never** passes out one night, call in your favorite tattoo artist. Apply something believable but hilarious to his bicep, like a rainbow. Have a matching tattoo drawn on your own bicep. When he wakes up and sees what is on his arm, tell him that late last night you both decided you wanted to get a tattoo as a reminder of what a great night you had, you know, to really hammer home that this was the best night of your lives.

Push Your Luck: Cry or freak out telling **Never** that you can't believe he made you do this. Now you are going to have to spend the rest of your life with a rainbow on your arm.

Prank Pitfall

You will have a Sharpie drawing of a rainbow on your bicep, too. That shit is hard to get off. Still, I didn't say it wasn't worth every scrub.

Invisible Skin

TARGET: Only Speaks Football

Tools *Saran Wrap*

This is a classic summer camp prank that works anywhere in which there are institutional toilets. Simply lift the toilet seat and spread the Saran Wrap so that it covers the mouth of the bowl. Replace the toilet seat and saunter out of the stall. Your target will be in for a surprise when he sits down for his morning constitutional.

Smeared

TARGET: Euro-Trash

Tools *Shaving cream, toothpaste, honey, or hair gel*

Place a dollop of the viscous substance of your choice on a sleeping **Euro-Trash**'s unsuspecting finger or a big clump into his palm. Then tickle him under the nose or on his forehead. He is guaranteed to smear whatever is on his hand all over his face.

Milking Human Kindness

TARGET: TA with the 'Tude

Tools

A phone

Call as many people in the university directory as you feel like calling and leave a message asking if they wouldn't mind going outside to look for your wallet. The funny part is that you are going to identify yourself as **TA with the 'Tude.** Leave his number and say you are calling from a nearby pay phone.

Up the ante by telling the person you are calling that there is a lot of money in that wallet. Mention that you know where the person lives and that you will be keeping a sharp eye on his expenses over the next few weeks. Let him know as well that if there is any unauthorized activity on your credit card you will not bat an eye before the proper authorities are notified. Continually call him "Bub," "Chief," or "Buster."

CYA

Call from a pay phone.

Final Blow

TARGET: Graveyard Goth

It turns out that **Grave-yard Goth** lives right next to the dorm study lounge. The night before finals, invite **Graveyard Goth** to come study for the Spooky Lit Final. Just as you turn to "The Tell-Tale Heart," silently phone her room. Call back over and over again if a machine interrupts the telephone ringing. When Goth gets home that night, it will surprise her to find her door kicked in and her phone cord torn from the wall. But that's what angry students with imminent finals do.

CYA

Make sure she doesn't have caller ID. Or use a special untraceable cell phone that will only lead **Goth** to a small fishing community in Morocco if she goes looking. (Not a bad investment for a true prankster.)

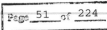

Switch Combs

TARGET: Sorority Spirit

Accomplice: Your competition for the love of Sorority Spirit

Tools

Two switch combs (also known as "switchblade combs")

The next time the Tri Delts host a party, you and your accomplice need to show up dressed like a couple of greasers circa 1950. When you ask **Sorority Spirit** for her number and she flat-out turns you down, turn to your buddy and say, "Is it because of you? She's going to the sock hop with you?" Your buddy should shrug and say, "So? What if she is?"

Now you have to escalate the fight. Because the thing about fights is that they are really entertaining for everyone. People will definitely stop to look as your voices rise.

Now, this is the best part. Reach into your back pockets and in one fluid motion, dramatically snap open your switch combs.

The best thing to have done before you arrive at the party is to choreograph your fight scene, like they do in the movies. In fact, watch a switchblade fight in a movie and mimic the steps (*West Side Story* or *Rumble Fish* have good examples). The only difference is that you should be using a switch *comb*, not a blade. At the last second, as you go in for the kill, really dramatically take the comb and run it through your hair, 1950s cool style. Your accomplice should then straighten up and do the same. Then both of you walk out together with a *Saturday Night Fever* swagger and maybe even a disco spin.

Criminal Behavior

TARGET: Smokes His Breakfast

Next time our buddy **Smokes** goes out, go into his room and knock everything over, pull things from drawers and generally make it look like someone was definitely looking for something. When he comes home he'll think he's been robbed. When he sees nothing's missing he'll wonder what "they" were looking for.

Push Your Luck: "Accidentally" leave a real-looking police badge or a Dunkin Donuts receipt somewhere in the room. With a stoner, there is no end to how far you can take the paranoia business.

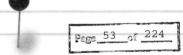

The Handlebar, the Van Dyke, the Pencil, or the Hitler

TARGET: Only Speaks Football

Tools
Sharpie

One night after a big game guarantees a big sleep for **Only Speaks Football**, it's time to break out the Sharpie again. This time, give this guy the sweet 'stache he could only *dream* of growing. Be it bushy or thin, loopy or classic, when he wakes up, only one thought will be in his head. "I totally deserve this."

Push Your Luck: Just let yourself draw. Once you've got the mustache on there, you probably won't want to stop. So keep going. Draw an Etruscan frieze on his calf, a landscape on his arm, and a Hello Kitty on his cheek. It's more about your pleasure than his displeasure, as are most things when you are in college.

Prank Pitfall

If you use a permanent marker, it's really hard to remove, so if your buddy has a job interview or a date with his dream girl, he might be really pissed. (That doesn't mean you shouldn't do it of course.)

Turn Left at the Popeye's Chicken

TARGET: Do-Gooding Hippie

If you see people looking lost somewhere on campus, feel free to volunteer your services to get them even lost-er. In particular, **Do-Gooding Hippie** just strikes me as someone really fun to do bad things to. So if you see **Do-Gooding** looking lost, run—don't walk—over to her and ask if you can help. When she asks where the Chem Lab is, give her the most incorrect directions possible. Send her straight off campus and to the fast food restaurant of your choice. Once she realizes that she's been led astray, you still won't be on the hook. Her bleeding heart will give you the benefit of the doubt and ultimately she will blame her own poor listening skills and elementary sense of direction. Isn't it fun to fuck with the hippies?

You can also try this with freshmen. As many as possible. Can you say "gullible"?

The Freshman Fifteen

TARGET: Euro-Trash

You know how your target has been spending a lot of time at the gym lately because of the cute dance major from his Greek Studies class? Now's the time to give him a little scare. Look at the brand name and size of **Euro**'s underwear and a favorite shirt and pair of jeans of his—or anything else you want to spend money on in the name of comedy that you can find in his wardrobe. Then go out and buy identical items one size smaller. (This prank works better and more cheaply if you already know someone smaller who has a similar wardrobe. Then you can just swap the clothes.) The prank begins when you ca-sually mention over dinner at the cafeteria that some girl you know literally blew up overnight. One day she fit in her clothes; the next day she could barely button her pants.

That night, when **Euro** is serenading his new obsession, swap out his underwear and clothes for the identical pieces in smaller sizes. The next day **Euro** will not know what happened when his underwear is too tight and his jeans won't button. But he will think back on the story from dinner and will likely skip breakfast.

The Chicken or the Egg

TARGET: President PompASS

<u>Tools</u>
Eggs

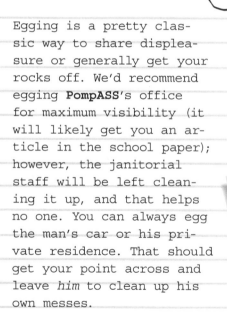

Egging is a pretty classic way to share displeasure or generally get your rocks off. We'd recommend egging **PompASS**'s office for maximum visibility (it will likely get you an article in the school paper); however, the janitorial staff will be left cleaning it up, and that helps no one. You can always egg the man's car or his private residence. That should get your point across and leave *him* to clean up his own messes.

Prank Pitfall

This is vandalism. If you get caught, and they **will** try to catch you, he will make you clean his home or his car or both.

CYA

Wear black, work at night, and hide well. Change your clothes before going home, and live off campus if possible.

Jilted Lover

TARGET: Backwards Baseball Cap

Tools

Campus voice mail

This prank requires that your school allow you to leave a voice mail for the whole campus. In some cases, this might require an accomplice who works in an administrative office where leaving all-campus voice mails is easy to do, or by stealing a faculty password. (A similar message can also be sent via all campus e-mail.)

If you are the one who got dissed by **Backwards Baseball Cap**, have a friend leave the message on your behalf. After all, you don't want to look crazy. Have the message say things like, "**Back-**

wards is no gentleman. He smells like talcum powder mixed with car exhaust and he has a lot of back fat." Also mention what a jerk he is to women.

Prank Pitfall

If the call is ever traced back to you, you will be that girl who left the message. This will either be a good thing or a very, very sad thing. So get a second, third, and fourth opinion before saving.

Chocolate Bath

TARGET: Sorority Spirit

Tools

Chocolate bath soap

Vinny

The latest craze in bath-time fun is soap that smells like food. That's what makes this prank so easy and fun. Give your girl, **Sorority Spirit**, a delicious-smelling present she will not be able to refuse. Empty a container labeled "chocolate bath soap" (Body Truffles makes one and so does Philosophy) and replace it with actual chocolate syrup. When you tell her it will make her smell delicious, you will not be kidding.

Push Your Luck: Mix real cream in with the chocolate. When she opens the lid to smell it when you give it to her it will smell great. But when she goes to use it a few days later the cream will have turned sour and it will smell disgusting!

Hell's Angels

TARGET: Everyone

Accomplices: A bunch of your toughest friends with their facial hair grown out and wearing black-leather biker outfits

First, go out and find an assortment of kids' bikes and junk bikes. Get them in acceptable riding order. Secondly, dress up with your accomplices as the dreaded "Scorpion" gang. Use duct tape to write out "Scorpions" with a logo on the back of your leather jackets. Have biker chicks on the handlebars, riding tandem, in sidecars, and on bicycles of their own. A few mean-looking dogs will also add to the over-all picture. Choose a day, preferably one of the first nice days of the spring, when a lot of people are outside. Then, ride into town on your ridiculous herd of bikes and trikes. Make sure you take your meanness seriously. Holler insults at the gawking crowd and flip a garbage can for good measure. Ride all over campus—then ride away.

Prank Pitfall

Someone might try to get you in trouble for flipping the garbage can. Take it like a man and flip him the bird.

Push Your Luck: Try to get an article in the school paper about a notorious biker gang known as the Scorpions wreaking havoc in neighboring counties. Mention that the last time anyone saw them they were headed "east" (or in the direction of your school).

XYZPDQ

TARGET: Anyone

This is an old standby but let me briefly remind you of the fun of "made ya look!" jokes. These can include such classics as "Were you born in a barn?" only to have the target look behind themselves at the self-closing door closing. Use "Your barn door's open!" on hot girls and nerdy guys whether or not their zipper is down. There's always the pointing at the chest joke that can look very suave if when the person looks down you skillfully flick their nose to knock their head back up. All these kinds of pranks are good practice rounds for later bigger jokier jokes. And practice makes perfect, which is a good collegiate lesson.

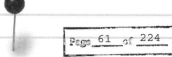

Dead Man Walking

TARGET: Limited Foresight

Accomplice: A few people "out for an evening stroll"

Tools

A bottle of pills, ketchup in a baggie, police tape, and chalk

One boring night ask your friend **Limited Foresight** if he wants to go for a walk around campus. While you walk, start a game where you kick stones back and forth. Pretend like one of the stones hits you hard in the head. Sit down and hold your head like you are in real pain. Have a little bit of ketchup in a bag in your pocket that you rub into your scalp. Ask **Limited Foresight** if he would run back to your room and get your pills. Tell him you have a low platelet count and since you are bleeding, it is a safety precaution. Assure him you're okay. You just bleed easily.

When he takes off to get the pill bottle you have left out on your dresser, draw a chalk figure of yourself on the ground like a dead person. Then rope the scene off with police tape and hide. Have two accomplices looking at the crime scene when he gets back tell him that some guy got bludgeoned to death with a rock and that he died. They can tell him the police are coming back, but they went with the body to the hospital.

Push Your Luck: Use extra ketchup. Leave some on the ground near where you "died." Make it look gruesome. A fake cop is a far better accomplice. One in uniform and one in a suit is even better. A small group of bystanders will make this prank hard to screw up.

Prank Pitfall

If **Limited Foresight** gets back too quickly from your room, he might not believe that the police came, drew the chalk line, took the body, and left the scene so quickly. Try to set the accident far enough away from your room that it will take **Limited** at least twenty minutes to get back.

Freezing Skivvies

TARGET: Only Speaks Football

Are you completely disgusted by the fact that this dude has not changed his underwear in the four weeks since his team went on the winning streak? The next time he strips down for bed, use tongs to transport that nasty set of boxers under the faucet and then once they're wet, into the freezer. The next morning, throw the boxers back where he left them and watch him try to put them back on.

Hellshire University

To: Harvard Medical School
RE: Pasty Library Geek

To Whom It May Concern,

While you know and are certain to trust my impeccable high opinion of the young Miss Geek, it doesn't mean you will automatically let her into your fine institution. I already explained to her that if she does not get in, it will not be because of my letter, but in fact because of her own limited performance. I did not tell her about the incident during which you "asked for my resignation." I put that experience out of my mind long ago. I understand that you had a choice to make, and since the girl's father was a dean, he had seniority. But let me just restate that I had no idea that she was underage, nor did I expect that she would be able to do *that* with a flashlight. Further, I continue to stand by my lecture during which I asserted that pi would have been calculated by now if it weren't for the morons in the administration of a certain school that begins with an H, who shall remain nameless, funneling money into idiot hobbies like Shakespeare and sports. But that is not the purpose of this letter. Rather, this letter is meant to show you that I have changed enough both as a man and as a professor *to have been asked* by a student to send you this letter of recommendation. As you see, I agreed although I remain tremendously busy. (However, if you would like another opportunity to discuss a potential tenured position with someone of my caliber I will be on or near your campus three to five days out of the week. This does not violate the restraining order. I looked into it.)

Once again, I recommend **Pasty L. Geek** for your superior medical school program. The more allies I have on the inside, the better.

Yours in Good Stead,

P. GASbAg

Professor Gasbag

Sophomore Pranks

Pranks for the Older but Still Largely Unwise

You metaphorically made it back for a second year, but only because your father paid someone off. Still, you think you are ready for pranks of a higher caliber. You aren't ready for the big guns, but you are ready for something that looks a little less desperate than talcum powder and shaving cream. Here you go. Just hope you have better hiding places this year!

Battle Balloon

TARGET: As many people as possible

Tools

Balloons filled with water and shaving cream

Set up a water fight on a warm day. You can either knock on doors, send out a big e-mail, or flier the campus to get people in on it. Or you can just go out to the quad with tons of balloons to share and start tossing.

After a little while, turn to someone and start the rumor that you heard some of those shaving cream balloons are filled with Nair or some other depilating/hair-removal cream. As the rumor spreads, watch the panic begin. Hilarious!

Prank Pitfall

People who actually believe they have been attacked with Nair might go to the police or otherwise make a big stink. Still, it's probably worth it for the laugh.

World Traveler

TARGET: Always Raises Her Hand

ACCOMPLICES: Anyone going on a vacation

Tools

A fake e-mail address, a lot of time, and a few upcoming vacations/vacationers

Once again, you are going to kidnap Mr. Snuffles, **Always Raises Her Hand**'s stuffed animal that she inevitably keeps on her bed. Send that monkey on as many adventures as you can to as many places as you can. Tell your accomplice it is for your sick little cousin. Ask him or her to photograph the little guy at famous locations then e-mail you the pictures. Then you forward the pictures on to **Always** without comment. When the monkey gets home from his tenth trip, return him to her with a pile of pic-tures and, if you are extra nice, a present from abroad.

Push Your Luck: Include an essay called "Mr. Snuffles Travels the World" with the pictures when you return the monkey. Put it in Mr. Snuffles's voice. She will find it hard not to be very amused.

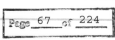

Plain-Clothed and Watching

TARGET: Smokes His Breakfast

Accomplice: A convincing person

Leak it to **Smokes His Breakfast** via your accomplice that you are actually a plainclothes cop trying to break down a huge drug ring. Make sure the accomplice emphasizes that you are not there to bother with petty criminals but you are taking notes on everyone you meet. It is a lot of fun to make stoners paranoid. If you've never tried it, this is your chance. See how he reacts to you now that he thinks you are watching him.

Prank Pitfall

*He might not want to hang out with you anymore. If he is your pot connection this might prove problematic for you. And it might be harder to convince him you are **not** a plainclothes cop trying to break down a huge drug ring.*

Flier, Flier, Pants on Fire

TARGET: Fire Crotch

Tools

*Pic of **Fire Crotch**, Photoshop or another drawing program, copy paper*

Once **Fire Crotch** has had her way with you then left you for dead, you might find yourself crying into a bottle of Maker's Mark. I'd like to suggest that instead of getting wasted, you get even!

Begin by Photoshopping a beautiful picture of our girl with her name beneath. Put a short list of ways she wronged you. Then copy the flier many times. One quiet night, paper the campus with them.

Prank Pitfall

If caught, you might be accused of stalking, harassment, or slander, all of which are illegal.

CYA

*Delete the picture and destroy any additional copies, then point your finger at another of Miss **Crotch**'s former conquests.*

Greek Tragedy #2

TARGET: Sorority Spirit

Tools

Faux letterhead

Spread the word that the campus sororities are going to be shut down due to excessively slutty behavior. Send paperwork from "The National Panhellenic/ Campus Liaison Committee" to **Sorority Spirit** explaining that due to improper behavior and documented cases of male visitors in the rooms past 10 P.M., the committee has no choice but to revoke the incorporation papers of the sororities of Hellshire University.

Push Your Luck: Convince **Sorority Spirit** to pass the letter on to the school paper accompanied by a letter of outrage.

Jack Frost

TARGET: Sorority Spirit

Tools

Baby powder and hair spray

Jesse

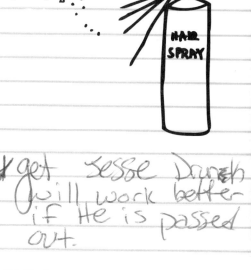

This prank can be done to anyone but is funniest with a vain person with dark hair who doesn't have time for a morning shower. One night after **Sorority Spirit** has passed out from hefty drinking (despite her 8 A.M. test), sprinkle baby powder in her hair and set it by spraying it with hair spray. It will take a long shower and several rounds of Pantene before it will come out. So, she might have to go take the test looking like Granny Spirit.

get Jesse Drunk will work better if He is passed out.

American Idol

TARGETS: Do-Gooding Hippie, Smokes His Breakfast, and Alterna-Chick

The next time you go ka-raoke, shyly admit to your targets that you've been thinking about trying to get on one of those reality TV singing shows. Tell them that you have always had this secret dream to be a rock star. You might also grease the wheels by letting them know that you have been told many times what a great voice you have.

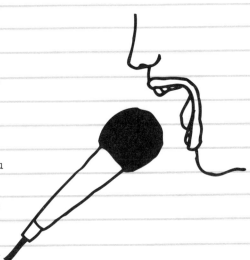

Now the key here is to be as incredibly earnest as you possibly can. *Do not laugh.* When you go up to sing "You Light Up My Life" or something by Kelly Clarkson, make sure you look like you are as serious as a heart at-tack. Also make sure you

belt that song out horribly. When you return to the table look hopefully at your targets waiting to see what they think. Tell them you want them to tell you the truth. Be crestfallen when they dash your dreams. If they don't, they are so not really your friends!

> **Tip:** You might want to plant one accomplice who will praise your singing with her whole heart. This will really confuse and worry your targets.

CD Madness

TARGET: Professor Buttons Unbuttoned

The lovely professor has just finished her second lecture of the day and has left her office vacant while she goes to get a manicure and pick up a pack of Marlboro Lights. You are waiting for her to get back and "help you" with your "paper," but she's really keeping you waiting. Go into her office and pull every CD and DVD out of its jewel case and switch them around. Then leave and go get lunch. You can always come back tomorrow.

Jazzy iPod

TARGET: Backwards Baseball Cap

Tools
Your target's iPod

Delete **Backward**'s iPod play
list and replace it with
easy listening and smooth
jazz selections. Ideas include Christopher Cross,
Bread, Neil Diamond (circa
1980), and Debbie Boone.

Prank Pitfall

*Your buddy learns to
really love Engelbert
Humperdinck and you are
forced to listen to him
repeatedly on the next
road trip.*

Pot the RA

TARGET: Anal RA

Tools
Weed seeds

The RA sure has been busting a lot of kids for pot lately. We recommend you go see him over an unrelated issue. When you are standing in his room, slip a few pot seeds into all the window plants and flowerpots in his room. He takes such good care of them it is certainly only a matter of time before those seeds grow into plants. Then we'll see who gets in trouble!

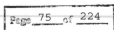

Psycho Shower

TARGET: Pasty Library Geek

<u>Tools</u>

Red fruit drink powder, wrench to remove showerhead

Craig

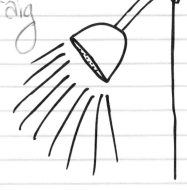

Remove the showerhead from the shower stall. Pack red fruit drink powder into the head. When **Pasty** turns on the water, she won't believe her eyes when it runs out bright red. Hopefully she won't go into convulsions. Although she may wonder if that's coming next!

Prank Pitfall

You will need to guard the shower to make sure it isn't wasted on some-body else. Oh wait. That wouldn't be a waste now, would it?

Water for Wine

TARGET: Never Drinks Water

Tools

Tinted wine or beer bottles, water

Empty an already-opened bottle of red wine from **Never Drinks**'s drink stash. Then refill the bottle with water mixed with a combo of red and blue food coloring until it roughly matches that of actual red wine. (Tinted bottles work best.)

Also try empty beer bottles. Fill them with water, wedge the lids back into place, and stick them in the fridge. Almost any bottle made out of colored glass will work. (Corona, for example, is an exception to this rule, since the bottle is made out of clear glass.)

Prank Pitfall

If you fill too many bottles of wine with water, you might run out of wine.

Freeze

TARGET: Everyone

Accomplices: As many as possible

This prank can be organized virally. Have an e-mail spread to as many people as possible that at a specific time on a specific day a group of people will be in the dining hall eating, or getting their food or socializing. At the agreed-upon time, these people will all freeze. Just completely freeze, for 120 seconds. They will not move a muscle. Anyone with no idea what is going on will likely wonder what's going on. After two minutes the prank will end and everyone will casually go back about their business, ignoring the fact that they were frozen for two minutes.

This prank will work at Spring Fling, Graduation, and any other event at which people gather. Agree to just shrug or act surprised if asked what happened.

Prank Pitfall

Organizing that many people is difficult. For this prank to work at least forty people need to agree to be a part of this, they can't move for two minutes, and they should be spread throughout the cafeteria. That's hard. Not impossible, but hard.

Phone Prank

TARGET: The cafeteria staff

Tools

A phone

Call the good folks work-
ing at the cafeteria and
with complete conviction
tell them you are a dog
breeder with too many lit-
ters. Tell them you will
butcher the animals and
mince the meat so no one
can tell what they are
eating. You will sell them
the butchered meat for
ninety-nine cents a pound.
Tell them that when mixed
with pork it is actually
quite tasty. Use arguments
like it being low in calo-
ries, tasting like chicken,
and great for helping out
their bottom line.

Tip: At the beginning of the call, avoid admitting what kind of meat you are selling for as long as possible.

The Lorax

TARGET: Do-Gooding Hippie

Accomplices: Two lumberjacks, a group of protesters, and a person to walk the target into the fray

Tools

Lumberjack duds, chain saws, poster board for protesters (optional)

Spread the word that the school has hired a group of lumberjacks to cut down the majestic oak on the academic quad. On the day of said cutting, organize a protest. Have two guys play the lumberjacks with chain saws and attitudes. Have a group of students surround the tree holding hands and singing songs of peace to create a convincing-looking protest. When **Do-Gooding Hippie** arrives, have her friend encourage her to join the protest. At some point, the lumberjacks need to go at the students with their

chainsaws in an attack. If the news media arrives, even better. Keep the prank going until the guys are about to cut down the tree and **Do-Gooding** is crying and hurling her body in front of the chainsaws. Then let her know it was all a joke. Hy-larious.

Washing the Pinks

TARGET: Limited Foresight

Tools

Pink clothes, red sock (optional, depending on how far you push it!)

Tell your roommate you are doing a few whites and ask if he has any to throw in. Several hours later, hand him back a pile of pink clothes. Apologize explaining a red sock was the culprit. At the end of this prank, you can either just give him back his still-white dirty clothes or, if he throws a huge fit and acts like a baby, throw his clothes away and let him live with the pinks.

Actually, you could really wash his whites with a new red sock, you know, for the hell of it.

Grannies, Lacies, and Thongs, Oh My!

TARGET: Only Speaks Football

<u>Tools</u>

Panties

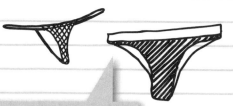

Break into your target's room when he is at a football game. Then pull all his underwear out of his underwear drawer, off his floor, and out of his laundry basket. Replace all of it with girls' underwear: mostly thongs. Then just play dumb.

URL Cruelty

TARGET: Creepy and Antisocial

<u>Tools</u>

A web URL

Set up a URL in your target's name and then post all kinds of unsavory facts about him. Feel free to include that he likes to sleep with a dead stuffed raccoon and that he cries easily.

Lousy Drunk

TARGET: Sorority Spirit

Tools

Blender, drink mixes, nonalcoholic bevvies

The next time you have a party, really give **Sorority** a chance to show off her true colors. Tell her you have some magic skills in the drink-making department. Serve her the fruit-iest, chocolat-iest, frou-frou-est drinks you can imagine. The punch line: There is no booze in there whatsoever. As you serve 'em up, make sure you mention how well **S.S.** holds her liquor! Four drinks in, spread the word that you've been serving up the drinks booze free as she drunkenly throws her arms around all the boys' necks and tries to feel up the girls on the dance floor.

CYA

Act like you had no idea that "root beer" and "grenadine" were nonalcoholic.

Prank Pitfall

She might not act drunk. But she probably will. The power of suggestion is strong with those girls.

Sunny Swears

TARGET: Fire Crotch

The next time **Fire Crotch** asks you to spread sunscreen on her for her afternoon rooftop tan, be prepared. First, coat her back and legs in baby oil or plain old lotion. Then write out swear words in sunblock down her legs and across her back. If you can get one on her chest, you get extra points. To get the words on there, act like you are just adding more lotion. Tell her you are playing a game and that she has to guess the word. She will enjoy this and think you are flirting. That is, until after her shower when she looks down at the back of her calves and sees, "bitch" and "asshole" written in sunshine.

CYA

Play innocent. Tell her you thought you were using the oil, not the sunblock. Blame dyslexia or bad eyesight.

Room for Rent

TARGET: Graveyard Goth

During the next Marilyn Manson concert, clean out your target's room as if she has moved out. When she gets home, her bed will be a mattress with no sheets and her drawers will all be empty. Hide her stuff wherever you can.

Push Your Luck: Set the room up like it is someone else's room entirely. Put different sheets on the bed, new clothes in the dresser, etc.

Door Soaker

TARGET: Divorced Old Guy

Tools

A garbage can, water

Lean a garbage can full of water up against your target's door. The next time he opens it, he will get soaked. So will everything behind him. Of course, this prank only works on doors that open inward. Doors that open *outward* will soak you, which you will deserve if you eff this one up.

Potty Mouth

TARGET: Smokes His Breakfast

Tools

A small piece of animal shit

Cut up a small piece of goat shit or cow patty into a cube. Give it to your target to smoke. When he inhales he will cough heartily. The punch line? "Wow, that must be some good shit!"

Cell Phone Changeup

TARGET: Will Do Anything to Get Some

One of the greatest all-time pranks requires no more than a cell phone left on a bar table while its owner excuses himself for a run to the restroom. The trick is to find the number of a girl he likes in the address book. Replace her number with your own number so whenever you text him, her name appears, and when she texts him, your name appears.

Prank Pitfall

This one usually ends badly: After all, who wouldn't get pissed when they've just planned out a whole ski trip or a late-night meet-up only to find out it was with some hairy asshole the whole time!

CYA

Play the victim. Blame someone else for switching your name with hers. Or switch an unrelated third party with the chick. No sense in calling attention to yourself unnecessarily.

Xbox Funeral

TARGET: Backwards Baseball Cap

Tools
Old Xbox   Kyle

Since **Backwards** will not step away from his Xbox, this one is perfect for him. Every Xbox user knows about "the red ring of death." When the green ring on an Xbox turns red, it means something is fried or otherwise broken for good. Find an old Xbox at a thrift store or use the one on your hall that has just crapped out. Swap it out with the Xbox-obsessed **Backwards**'s one day when his girlfriend forces him out to the latest *Sex and the City* movie. I guarantee something very close to tears when he sees his precious Xbox with the red ring of death.

Push Your Luck: Have a funeral for the sad little Xbox. Just before you go to bury it, come clean. He'll be so happy to have his precious baby back, he may even let the whole thing go. (Yeah right.)

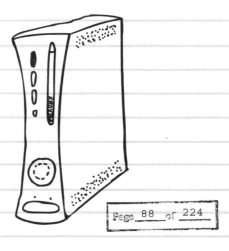

Five-Oh, Be Cool

TARGET: Sorority Spirit

Accomplice: At least one person needs to dress up with you

Tools

Cop getup

At the next big Tri Delt party show up dressed as cops. Stand around looking serious. Don't say anything. Finally, pour yourself a drink from the keg and walk out the door.

Prank Pitfall

If this happens too close to Halloween, no one will believe you. But if you pick a random date and grow the appropriate facial hair, it will be very funny!

The Breakup

TARGET: Euro-Trash

Accomplice: Your significant other

At **Euro**'s big graduation blowout at the dance club rented out by his father, the Count, you and your girlfriend should show up already engaged in some kind of dramatic fight. The best way to pull this off is to have a preselected fight topic: For example, you are angry because she has gone to one too many "office hours" with her hot physics teacher. Stage the fight in multiple locations around the party. Include yelling, drink tossing, and crying if possible.

Push Your Luck: Get up on the stage after the father makes his speech in Greek and English telling his son how proud he is. Take the microphone and wish **Euro** great luck taking over his father's business and lament your own lack of a future. Then end the toast by thanking your girlfriend for trading you in for a better model. Down your drink and receive your escort from the club with "grace" (in other words, cry like a baby).

Desperately Seeking Lovin'

TARGET: Will Do Anything to Get Some

This prank is Old School, but its nostalgia factor is a large part of its charm. Take out a classified ad in your school paper with your target's e-mail or phone number attached. Try: SWM seeks SF, all sizes welcome! Must love moonlit walks, Engelbert Humperdinck, and roller-blading in spandex.

If your school paper doesn't have a classifieds section, investigate how much it will cost to buy an ad advertising the general "services" of **Will Do Anything**. If you get a group of people to invest in the ad, the hilarity of the prank might be equal to or exceed the cost.

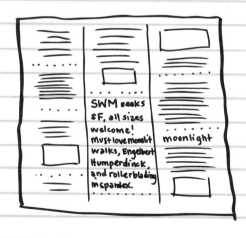

Desktop Madness

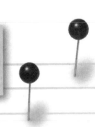

TARGET: Always Raises Her Hand

One day while your target is volunteering at the hospital, go onto her private computer. Hit "print screen" on her desktop. Open PowerPoint and right click to paste. That way you will have a saved picture of your target's desktop. Save the picture as wallpaper. Hide the toolbar and all the icons so it looks exactly like her desktop. The heart of this prank is that nothing opens no matter what she clicks on. When she calls for IT help, she is in for some serious humiliation.

Push Your Luck: Do the above prank at the computer lab to all of the university computers. If you do it around finals, prepare to hide out for a while afterward.

April, as in Fools

TARGET: Your parents

Tools

A phone

Call your parents and tell them that you and your significant other are having a baby. Explain that your partner is Catholic and completely opposed to abortion. Continue to milk the story until your parents are sufficiently hooked. Finally end the prank by saying, "We decided to name her April, as in Fools."

CYA

You won't have to. This is one story your parents will be happy you lied about.

A Condom Full

TARGET: Only Speaks Football

Tools

A condom

Devan

Fill a condom with as much water as it will hold (unreliable sources say that it will hold nearly five gallons). Move it carefully in a gently cradled blanket and place it on your target's bed. (If you fill the condom on the bed it might burst prematurely, and we all know what that's like....)

When **Football** discovers his fun present, he is certain to break it all over his bed with no more than the simple action of lifting it up. Something at which he is likely experienced.

Putting the *Hand* in *Handicapped*

TARGET: Greek Asshole

Is there some part of your body that is a little off? A fucked-up nose? An unsightly birthmark? Does **Greek Asshole** make nasty comments about it? Of course he does. This prank turns it around on the asshole. The next time he gives you shit for, say, your chewed-up ear, run off and cry. Make a big show of it. Have an accomplice turn to your target and tell him that he should lay off. The ear is the result of a really bad car accident a few years ago in which your little sister died.

Your boy **Greek** will inevitably feel terrible. You will be promised that no one will ever make fun of your ear again, and if they do, he will set them straight!

For the next four years you might be surprised how many dick moves you get away with because everyone feels bad about your sister and your ear.

CYA

If anyone comes home to your parents' house, remark that it's really hard for them to even think about your sister. That's why there are no pictures. At graduation, feel free to come clean.

Toothbrush Hostage

TARGET: Greek Asshole

Tools
A camera or camera phone

Steal the target's tooth-brush and take pictures of the toothbrush washing the toilet basin. Replace the toothbrush. A few days later, send **Asshole** the pictures of his toothbrush in the toilet bowl. Then wait for your beat-down.

Scrub-a-dub-dub

Tour Kidnap

Accomplice: A hot girl and a few people to assist in the kidnapping

Tools

Black clothes, black makeup, ski masks (optional)

Plant your hot girl in a tour group of prospective students. As the tour group rounds a corner, you and your accomplices wearing black with black raccoon paint around your eyes should run up yelling, "SHE'S OURS AND WE'RE TAKING HER BACK!"

Even better—dress up in sweatshirts of a rival school and wear ski masks.

Push Your Luck: Film the expressions of the tour group for later perusal.

Tardy Hardy

TARGET: Always Raises Her Hand
Accomplice: Always's roommate

After the most recent 9:00 P.M. request for quiet from your target, you have decided that enough is enough. One night have the roommate set her clock ahead two hours. Also change any visible clocks in hallways or on the dorm lounge VCR. When **Always** gets up at 4 A.M. instead of her usual 6 A.M., she likely won't realize a thing until she gets to the caf for her morning oatmeal with raisins and finds it still closed.

Prank Pitfall

If your target checks her phone or computer before getting out of her pajamas the whole thing might backfire.

Runaway Train

TARGET: Never Drinks Water

Tools

Vacuum cleaner

One night before your target goes into a deep passed-out state, set up a vacuum cleaner at the foot of his bed (ideally the old-fashioned uprights with lights work loudly and best). Whisper to your target, "The airplane's crashing, the airplane's crashing...." (Alternatively, chant something about a train coming.)

Then turn on the vacuum and run it up his body, moving it quickly toward his head.

Dressed the Statue

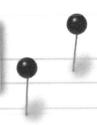

TARGET: Professor Buttons Unbuttoned

Tools

Stolen items from your target and a wig

Every school has a great statue of a president or one of its founders somewhere on campus. For this prank you are going to dress the statue. Over time, steal items of clothing from your target's car and office. Whatever you can get. A winter hat, a jacket, a skirt. Then one day dress the statue using the clothing, a wig that matches your professor's hair, and one item of hers that will make the likeness unmistakable (like a book she wrote or a plant she brings to class to give the room a little life).

Prank Pitfall

No one knows who the statue is supposed to be. (But it's still funny to dress it, so no one loses.)

Pee Break

TARGET: Do-Gooding Hippie

Tools

Bowl large enough to fit your target's hand comfortably

Vinny

Once you have had it with your target never flushing the toilet in her misguided attempts to save the earth, wait until she is sleeping. This slumber party favorite still works in college. Once she is definitely sound asleep, gently place her hand in warm water. In all probability she will pee in her bed. If this doesn't teach her a lesson, pour out her soy milk and replace it with evil inorganic whole milk.

Prank Pitfall

She might not pee and will just have a wet hand. Then it's a lame prank.

Butler Conveyer

TARGET: The cafeteria staff and students

Tools

Tuxedo

Dress up in a tuxedo with your hair slicked back. Now, holding two trays full of dirty dishes, ride the conveyer belt meant for dirty dishes into the dish room. Hand off the trays and continue back around to the front. Take more trays from anyone about to set his tray down. See how many times you can go around before you are escorted out of the dining hall.

CYA

Hire an actor to pull off the prank on your behalf. He can claim he was hired. No one will get in trouble, as he will be a victim of the prank himself.

Dye Job

TARGET: Euro-Trash

Tools
Blue hair dye

The only thing those European students love more than their scooters is their thick head of black hair. One night tell **Euro** you are noticing a few grays in his gorgeous locks. Tell him you studied cosmetology before college and you'll dye his hair for him. Dye his hair bright blue using a wash-out dye that coats hair and can be used on all hair colors. He will freak out at first, but when it washes out easily he might forgive you before he takes back the invite to his family yacht in Cannes for spring break.

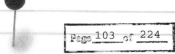

Vanity Homes and Gardens

TARGET: Everyone

Tools

Stapler and glue

Go to the library late one night and pull all the magazines off the rack. Carefully remove their covers and replace them with other magazine covers using either the stapler or the glue. Then put everything back where it was.

CYA

Hide from the surveillance cameras.

Just D

TARGET: Fire Crotch

Tools

White frosting, olive oil

Replace your target's shampoo with honey and her
conditioner with white
frosting loosened with water. See how long it takes
her to figure out that her
hair is being prepped for
dessert, not cleaned for
Friday night.

   Or if she's drunk enough,
replace her shampoo with
olive oil. The consisten-
cy will be wrong, but she
might just put it straight
into her hair and ac-
complish the opposite of
cleaning it.

Egg in

TARGET: Lim

Tools

...ted Foresight

...gs

Since this is the jerkoff that totaled your car after you loaned it to him, it is certainly time for payback (now that he's out of the hospital and off the crutches). Place eggs with small cracks in them into the shoes of your target. When he gets dressed the next day and puts them on, he won't know it, but he'll be helping to prepare breakfast.

Prank Pitfall

He might see the eggs before he puts his shoes on and will remove them before the prank begins. Next time, put them in his boots.

American Graffiti

TARGET: Will Do Anything to Get Some

Tools

A Sharpie

Find out which class your
target has with his crush.
Then gather information
about that crush. Graffiti
all over your target's face
and body the night be-
fore his final while he is
sleeping with information
like "Hates Italians" (if
she's Italian) and "HUGE
Red Sox fan!" (if she likes
the Yankees), etc.

Prank Pitfall

*He might skip the final in
order to kick your ass.*

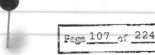

Casting Call

TARGET: Never Drinks Water

Tools

Plaster, gauze, and water

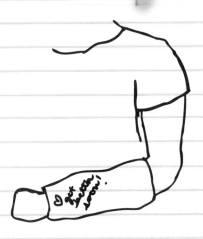

One night when your target passes out from drinking, put a plaster cast on his arm. In the morning tell him he got into a fight and broke it. Make up an elaborate story about a trip to the hospital. See how long he keeps the cast on before figuring out that his arm isn't actually broken at all.

Push Your Luck: Do it close to vacation so that he goes home to his parents wearing an unnecessary cast.

Prank Pitfall

If you put the cast on incorrectly, you could stop circulation in the poor kid's arm and cause permanent damage. That will probably not be funny.

Midterm

You've made it halfway. Now we must test your prankster wherewithal to see if you are earning your rep.

1. At what temperature do you bake a cream pie?

a. 350 degrees F
b. 450 degrees F
c. 12 degrees C
d. None of the above.

2. What nation hosts the biggest annual tomato fight?

a. The United States
b. Tomatonia
c. Brazil
d. Spain

3. Who is the originator of the whoopee cushion?

a. Sam Adams (of S.S. Adams, a famous gag and joke firm circa 1930—not the founding father or the beer)
b. David Hasselhoff (of G.G. Hasselhoff, a famous gag and joke firm circa 1870—not *Knight Rider!*)
c. Howard Hughes (*the* Howard Hughes of TWA circa 1935)
d. Herbert Hoover (as in the thirty-first U.S. president) when he was in high school, circa 1890

4. When using a fake British accent, what is the best pronunciation for "potato chips"?

a. Po-TAY-toe cheep
b. Crisps
c. Cheeps
d. Pah-tah-tow cheep

5. Which of the following makes the best fake blood?

a. Red Jell-O mixed with water
b. Fire-engine red nail polish mixed with nail polish remover to thin
c. A combination of honey, cornstarch, red food coloring, and flour
d. Pig's blood

6. What school pulled off the Great Rose Bowl Hoax of 1961?

a. UCLA
b. University of Minnesota
c. MIT
d. Caltech
e. University of Washington

7. Who would be the funniest person to ask for when making a prank phone call?

a. Debbie Morganstein
b. Marc Newman
c. John Jones
d. Ivanna Tinkle

8. Which TV show is *not* an example of a show about pranks?

a. *Candid Camera*
b. *Crank Yankers*
c. *Punked*
d. *Dunked*

9. On what day does April Fool's Day fall?

a. April 1
b. April 21
c. March 31
d. May 1 (at Midnight)

10. What did the BBC say "Smelovision" was in a 1965 prank on its viewers?

a. A medical breakthrough that would help people with poor senses of smell to instead *see* smells.
b. A new technology that would allow the transmission of odor over the airways to its viewers.
c. A way for blind people to see using the sense of smell as a guide.
d. A type of candy that you eat through your nose.

Answer Key

1/d (You don't bake a cream pie, you buy a premade crust and whip the cream then pour it in cold); 2/b; 3/a; 4/b; 5/c (if you answered "d" you are wrong because pig's blood is real blood); 6/d; 7/d; 8/d; 9/a; 10/b.

Score

Take a percentage: 1 right is 10 percent, 2 right is 20 percent, 3 right is 30 percent . . . 9 right is 90 percent, and 10 right is 100 percent.

0–50 percent: F—Retake the class.

60 percent: D—At least you showed up, even if you slept through most of it.

70 percent: C—Average.

80 percent: B—You are on your way.

90–100 percent: A—Your parents would be proud.

Junior Pranks

Pranks for Those with Off-Campus Housing

You've been at school for a couple of years now. You know your way around campus. You recognize more than twenty people by sight. You can probably even sing along to a song or two of the campus's favorite band. Now it's time to start really flexing the muscles that are finally taking the place of your baby fat, or the Freshman Fifteen.

World's Largest Jell-O Mold

TARGET: Everyone

Tools

Stuff to make a tub for the Jell-O, tarp or thick plastic, a few boxes of Jell-O (to get things started)

Spread the word that the *Guinness Book of World Records* is coming to campus to see if you can pull off the world's largest pile of Jell-O. One way to give the prank some believability is by constructing a tub in which to place the Jell-O out of a wooden frame lined with a tarp or thick plastic. Ask everyone to make Jell-O and bring it out to the quad starting at noon on a particular Sunday. Spread the word via e-mail, flier, and word of mouth. Watch the pile grow. When everyone starts looking around for the Guinness people, play dumb. Finally, when it is clear the Guinness people aren't coming, start a Jell-O fight.

Prank Pitfall

People may not get into the spirit of the thing, and you might only end up with a Jell-O ant hill instead of a Jell-O mountain. And that's embarrassing for you.

College Dropout

TARGET: Your parents

Tools

University letterhead

Send your parents a letter on university letterhead letting them know that their tuition payment for the semester will be sent back to them expeditiously (it is good to use big words when faking letters). Include something similar to: "We are sorry our school did not meet the expectations of your son and hope that after he takes some time, he will return to the school with a more focused and refreshed outlook. A spot will be saved for him in the class of (insert the year after the year you were expected to graduate)."

CYA

When they call to ask what's going on, you can either tell them you don't know anything about that letter and let them "look into it further." Or you can just come clean. They will be so glad you didn't drop out, they'll probably think it's funny.

Date Night

TARGET: Will Do Anything to Get Some
Accomplice: A hot girl, a date for you

Tell the target that your hot cousin is visiting and she really wants to be set up on a date. You will double with them so it isn't awkward. Make sure you mention that your cousin is a little weird—she does this thing with codes. If her date responds to the code correctly, she has made a promise to herself that she will perform all kinds of nasty acts on that lucky guy. But the code is really complicated and it is unlikely anyone could crack it. When he pressures you to give him the answers to it, don't give in right away, make him beg you for it, maybe even pay you!

The code has three parts. Tell him if she orders spaghetti at dinner and then complains that it is cold, it is a sign that she likes him. In response, he has to call the waiter over and complain that her spaghetti is too cold and make him replace it with a fresh plate; that way, she knows he is considerate. Later if she mentions that she loves the music playing, it means she is having a great time, so he should get up and dance to whatever the music is; that way, she knows he is a good listener. If at the end of the date she *really* likes him and wants to go home with him, she will say, "I have to get up early tomorrow, so we better call it a night." Now is the tricky part. He must climb up on the highest point possible (if he's at a restaurant or bar, he should get on a chair or table; if he's outside, he should get on a bench or up some stairs) and howl at the moon—*loudly*! He should be trying to wake the neighborhood with his wild baying. This will let her know that he really, really wants her.

CYA

When she runs like the wind **away** from him and he turns to you to ask what gives, tell him you must have gotten the last one wrong. Be nonchalant, saying maybe he was supposed to buy her flowers or something. Tell him better luck next time and walk away with your (likely impressed and well entertained) date.

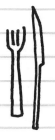

Exam Earthquake

TARGET: Professor Gasbag

This trick comes in handy if you find yourself late handing in a take-home final. As everybody knows, you can answer the questions to a take-home final anywhere, but you must hand it back in by a certain time. When you arrive at **Gasbag**'s office to hand in your exam late, he will shrug as he shuffles all the on-time papers on his desk and tells you no dice.

So you ask him, "Don't you know who I am?"

Of course he won't know what to say. But you know that he has no idea what the names are of the more than 300 people in his class.

So you will repeat, more aggressively and moving forward, "I said, don't you know who I am?"

When he says no, grab the stack of papers with yours in your hand, throw the whole pile up in the air, then run out of the office.

Push Your Luck: If you want to pull off this joke for the joke's sake and not your GPA's sake, choose a professor of a class you are not taking. Do the joke as written above except if you get "caught" and are told you will fail you can just shrug and say, "I didn't take the class anyway, so that's cool."

Prank Pitfall

This prank is best pulled off during finals of your senior year by someone with no interest in returning to campus for graduation, just to play it safe.

Keg Stand

TARGET: Greek Asshole

Tools

Keg of root beer

The next time Phi Sig organizes a kegger, replace one of the kegs with a keg of root beer (*www.kegof rootbeer.com*). Announce that this is a new type of beer. It's very sweet. See how long it takes for the partygoers to notice that what they're drinking isn't making them loopy—they are just like that naturally.

CYA

After laughing at the lame people for a while and spiking your root beer with ice cream, leave the party. That's just a tip. At frat parties, people really like their alcohol.

From the Well

TARGET: Backwards Baseball Cap

<u>Tools</u> *Vinny*

A bucket full of water

This prank is too easy and, frankly, a classic. When your target leaves the room, balance a bucket of water on top of a doorjamb. This is best achieved by having the door slightly ajar so that it makes an "A" shape with the wall and can successfully lean open and balance the bucket. When the target returns and pulls the door open a shower will ensue.

Prank ~~Pitfall~~ Pitfall

Everything within fifteen feet will get wet, so you might want to leave the room before he gets back.

Graduation Rumble

TARGET: Everyone

Accomplices: As many as you can rally

As the graduates and their families sit listening to as many boring speakers as the school can find to ego-stroke, set up a trigger such as a fight between a girl and a guy in a cap and gown. All of a sudden, multiple fights should erupt. They should be scheduled to last one minute and then abruptly stop. When the ceremony goes on, no one will have any idea what happened. But it's going to be funny!

Push Your Luck: Add a prop like food, silly string, or squirt guns.

CYA

The more fights going on, the harder it will be for security to stop it. Ideally, get the whole class in on it.

Haunted Bathroom

TARGET: The girls

Accomplices: Two to five people to get everything going at the same time

Tools

Blue and neon light bulbs, a portable stereo, lipstick, red juice drink powder, Vaseline

The truth is, there are few places scarier than institutional bathrooms. First of all, there is the buzzing of the green-hued fluorescent lights. There is the long row of bathroom stalls and shower stalls, which means plenty of places for the creepy and just plain scary to hide. Then of course, there are mirrors.

This prank requires a modicum of setup. Begin by setting up a few blue/neon lights in different places around the bathroom. The plug-in kinds use outlets and are independent of the light switch. Have one strobe light ready to go as well. Smear Vaseline on the mirrors so that when they steam up, messages appear. (You can also use red lipstick for messages; however, steam is creepier.) Music is a great added touch. It can either just be loud and disorienting or soft and spooky. Now, wait until a few girls are in the shower. Then turn on all the black lights. Turn on each of the faucets and at the same time, flip the light switch off and turn on the music and the strobe light. Then hide and watch the mayhem that ensues.

Unveil this prank slowly until people begin to wonder if this bathroom is haunted. Start with the subtlety of a message written in steam, for example write the name of a student that died at the school with the date of her death: Hilda MacEnerny 1962. One day, when someone is in the shower, play a song from 1962, softly, so that the person can't be sure where the music is coming from. Occasionally reach in and flip off the lights. Put in blue/neon lights and graffiti the walls in invisible messages like: "Help!" and "I'm dying!" so that when the lights are flipped off and the blue/neon lights are switched on, the terrifying messages are revealed.

You will be sure to terrify the crap out of the users of that bathroom. And since this is college, you have plenty of time to create your own mythology. Milk it!

Drive-Through Racket

TARGET: Everyone

Tools

Paper and tape

One day at the drive-through, order your burgers, fries, and drinks, then slap a sign over the speaker saying, "Speaker Broken. Please Yell." Then collect your meal, park in the lot, and sit back for a little dinner theater.

Disappearing Class

TARGET: Professor Buttons Unbuttoned
Accomplices: Professor Gasbag and the rest of the class

This one is part prank, part magic trick. One particularly restless day, have your professorial accomplice knock on the classroom door and call **Buttons** out of the room. When she is gone, have everyone leave their things exactly as they are and "disappear" into **Gasbag**'s classroom. When your target comes back to the room, you are all missing. She will look around for you back in the hall but won't see you. Wait a few minutes. Have your accomplice return a few minutes later. Have him lead her away saying that he thinks he saw her class down the hall. While **Buttons** is distracted, return to your seats as if nothing happened. When she comes back, act like you never left. When she presses you to answer where you've been, make fun of her. Give her answers like, "Maybe we were abducted by aliens" or "I think we were in a parallel universe!" Then laugh your ass off at her until she just goes on with the lesson, perplexed and flummoxed.

Prank Pitfall

Your target might catch you mid-move if your accomplices suck and don't move fast enough.

Rock Star

TARGET: Sorority Spirit

Tools

University letterhead

First spread the word that Coldplay is planning a college tour. Next, tell the target that your dad just happens to work for EMI, the group's new label. Tell them that you think you can book them for their (insert name of idiot dance spectacle—i.e., the Valentine Sock Hop) if she can get all the girls in the house to write letters to Coldplay telling them why they should come play their college-sponsored event. Hand the letters all over campus.

   Tip: Ideally you should find an accomplice doing an internship at EMI. Have him send a correspondence back and forth with someone else at the company to give your prank authenticity. The most recent e-mail in the thread should be from "your dad" to you saying that it's looking promising. A few weeks later tell the Tri Delts that the tour's been cancelled.

Push Your Luck: Tell the ladies you have an awesome replacement band. Then, the night of the sock hop, show up with your Spinal Tap–esque band. If you know a crappy polka band you can hire, even better!

Twitter Is for Suckahs

TARGET: Always Raises Her Hand

Get a hold of your tar-
get's twitter password and
log on to her page. Make
a list of tweets and sta-
tus updates describing an
intimate activity and post
them one at a time, one
per minute. Start with:

He just opened me up and went right in.

(Wait sixty seconds.)

I am really enjoying the way he gets all the way to the back.

(Wait another sixty seconds.)

I feel like he is completely releasing everything dirty inside of me. Cleaning it all out. Good.

(Wait sixty seconds.)

Too bad every dentist appointment ends in a bill.
(Ba-da bump.)

Dirty Rotten Scoundrel

TARGET: Your next-door neighbor

Accomplice: Your next-door neighbor's girlfriend

One day when your next-door neighbor is definitely home, you and your accomplice should pretend to be having great sex, loudly. Throw things around, do a little screaming and lots of rhythmic banging. Ten minutes later, his girlfriend should go knock on his door. When he asks where she's been or what she's been doing, she should casually say she's been next door helping you do a little redecorating. Hopefully, he'll forgive you when he finds out it's all a joke—hopefully.

Prank Pitfall

He might not believe you, will break up with his girlfriend, and then proceed to beat your face in. Or she will, for convincing her to be a part of such a lame prank.

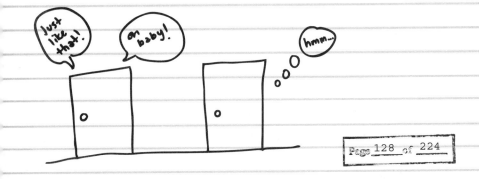

Underwear Up the Flagpole

TARGET: Always Raises Her Hand

Tools

Clothespins and frozen clothing

This old faithful is a classic. For best results, perform it in the dead of winter. Steal several items of clothing (five to ten) and wet them. Stick them out a window to freeze them so they stick out straight. The next night, using clothespins, run them up the flagpole. When your target sees her pink lace bra next to her Hello Kitty pajamas, it is possible her head will explode. But everyone else will be grateful for the laugh.

Alien Abduction

TARGET: Your roommate and friends

Tools

Green, slimy substance; probe-like tool

This prank is most convenient for you if you time it just before you go on a weeklong cruise with your family. First of all, avoid mentioning anything about a family cruise. Now, set the stage. Make your bed look slept in but abandoned. Leave a little green slime on your pillow and somewhere on the bottom sheet. Also, leave some kind of probe-like tool somewhere near the scene. Then simply disappear. Let your friends draw whatever conclusions they will.

Tip: The cruise plan is good because your cell phone won't work and you will have limited access to e-mail and telephone. But if you choose another time when you are away from school be sure to turn off your cell phone and avoid the Internet or you might get caught.

Push Your Luck: Shine a huge light into your window long enough to wake your roommate. Then turn it off and disappear quickly.

The *New York Times*

TARGET: TA with the 'Tude
Accomplice: As many people from his classes as possible

Tools

A phone

Call your target and tell him that you are with the *New York Times*. You are interested in doing an article on him for his work in (insert appropriate field of study). Emphasize that you are running on a very short deadline. Set up an appointment to meet him in his office at a certain time. At the planned time, show up with as many people as you can begging for help with class work. No matter how many times he asks you to leave, or wait until later, *do not leave*. Continue asking questions for about an hour. If you want to give the prank closure, have the *Times* leave a message saying they tried to find him but the line outside his door was too long. Let him know that he shouldn't worry because **Professor Gasbag** fielded the interview instead.

> **Tip:** The phone you use should be a New York City number or it's going to be pretty suspect. If the target calls the number later, the phone's owner should insist his phone was stolen on the day **TA** claims to have been called. For the sake of the prank, maybe it really *was* stolen.

Sugar for Salt

TARGET: Cafeteria eaters

Accomplice: Someone on the cafeteria staff to let you in during off-hours

Switch all the saltshakers with the sugar dispensers. It sounds easy, but it's a really bitchy thing to do and you will then have to live with yourself.

Push Your Luck: Switch all the salt and sugar in the pantry so that the food itself is *prepared* incorrectly. You can do the same thing with the powdered sugar and the flour as well.

CYA

Block out the cameras before beginning this prank. You also might want to murder your accomplice before he calls out your sorry ass to save his own.

Asleep in the Quad

TARGET: Never Drinks Water

Accomplice: Someone to help you carry a bed with an occupant

After another night of tying one on, move your target's bed out of his dorm room with him passed out in it. Leave him in the middle of the quad. It will be very funny in the morning.

Prank Pitfall

If it is wintertime and very cold, this is a very stupid prank and you are a supreme asshole for even considering it.

Craig
&
Vinny
&
Kyle

Toilet Paper Shortage

TARGET: Do-Gooding Hippie

Accomplice: Anal RA

Tools

Paper, Sharpie, jar

Post a sign in the girl's bathroom on university letterhead saying that due to cutbacks in spending, the school will no longer provide toilet paper. Instead, the students will be required to contribute to a toilet paper fund in the amount of one dollar per week. Beneath the sign leave a large jar with the words, "Toilet Paper Fund" in bold black letters. At the end of the sign include **Anal RA**'s phone number. When your target sees the sign she will immediately get on her soapbox and call your accomplice. When she calls him to rip him a new one, he will apologize and tell her it is not his fault. Then he will tell her she has to discuss it with the janitorial staff. I advise you to get him directions to their offices to pass to the target. When she goes there to let her head spin in their office, they are guaranteed to laugh their asses off at her.

Who knows—you might get a few bucks in the T.P. Fund too!

Push Your Luck: Let the janitorial staff in on it. Have them send **Do-Gooding** to another office where another member of the staff will send her someplace else until finally she is sent back to the dorm where you can reveal that the whole thing is a prank. Awesome.

Rock and Roll Fantasy

TARGET: Everyone

Tools

Water balloons (optional)

Spread the word that you heard some big band was coming to campus to test out a few songs for a long-awaited new album. Keep it vague. Then slowly leak rumors about it, like you heard it was the Beastie Boys or the Roots. Make signs to publicize the event with a specific date and time. On the day of the event, bring at least twenty people to stand there looking at a building or a statue or whatever. People will come. Tell them to wait with you. Fill the quad. Ten minutes after the designated meeting time, leave and go home.

Push Your Luck: Come armed with water balloons and start a balloon free-for-all.

Record Books

TARGET: Professor Gasbag and the whole student body
Accomplice: Someone to call your phone during the prank

Tools

A phone

Tell your target that the *Guinness Book of World Records* is coming in order to attempt to fill a single classroom with the most students possible. Ask if you can use his room. Next, organize as many people under the same premise to attempt to fit into the room. If you get press there, you get extra points for personal greatness. As the room is filling, answer a call and tell the room that the rep is just now looking for parking and will be at the location any minute. Continue adding people. Once you have a room full of people stuffed in there, field a final phone call. When you hang up, act a little upset as you tell the room that the *Guinness* representative went to the wrong place and now has to reschedule for next month.

CYA

Just keep blaming Guinness. Boycott the beer of the same name even though it's an unrelated company for extra passionate effect.

New Room

TARGET: Creepy and Antisocial

One night when **Creepy** the suitemate from hell is off polishing his knife collection, take all of his furniture and belongings and set them up in the hallway. Make it look like that is going to be his new room. If possible, mimic his setup perfectly, from the placement of his life-size poster of the Unabomber to his *Star Trek* figurines still in boxes on his bookshelf. Then carry on with your life as if nothing out of the ordinary has happened.

Become Her Ob-Gyn

TARGET: Alterna-Chick

Steal your target's cell phone and switch your number with the number for her gynecologist. It will be very weird for her if she calls to set up an appointment and gets you. Weirder still if she calls to hang out with you and gets her gynecologist.

Trash Barrels of Fun

TARGET: Anyone in your dorm

<u>Tools</u> *Vinny*
Barrels full of water

Fill with Marbles
lean & run

Lean trash barrels of water up against the elevator doors. When the doors open, everyone on the elevator gets soaked.

Push Your Luck: Think about it. What else can you fill those trash barrels with? This prank isn't called "Trash Barrels of Fun" for nothing!

Killer Traffic

TARGET: The campus at large

Accomplices: One person to hit and one person to help you throw the body in the trunk

Tools
A car

Driving on campus one day, fake-hit a friend with your car. Get out of the car, open your trunk, and throw him into it. Drive off. Squealing brakes help this prank markedly.

Prank Pitfall

Careful you don't actually hit anyone.
Because that would suck.

London Calling

TARGET: Only Speaks Football

If your dorm is anything like most other dorms in America, it has drop ceilings. Those fancy industrial rectangles made out of lightweight tiles are the perfect place for hiding a lot of things, but nothing more hilarious than a cell phone. Steal your target's phone and push up one of the tiles in order to set the phone on top of the adjacent tile. Next call the phone. Then watch as the dude tears apart his room looking for it. The drop ceiling will be the last place he'll look.

Quad Skating

TARGET: The whole campus

Tools

A hose, ice skates

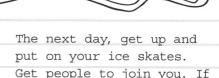

Flood the quad in the middle of winter. Use any abandoned hose next to any building on the quad—or go to a local hardware store and buy one on sale.

The next day, get up and put on your ice skates. Get people to join you. If the dean doesn't have you arrested, maybe it will become an annual event!

You Smell Like Roses!

TARGET: Only Speaks Football

Tools

Grandma perfume or super smelly essential oil

Swap out your target's Axe body spray or favorite cologne for some super flowery perfume. You could also just add a flowery-smelling essential oil (you can buy them at Victoria's Secret, the Body Shop, and a lot of other places) to his lotions or shampoos.

Dirty Blood

TARGET: Sorority Spirit

Tools

Fake letterhead

Next time your school hosts a big blood drive, see if this cute target will go with you. Usually the blood drives are sponsored by local hospitals. You can use the hospital website to make letterhead and draft **Sorority Spirit** a "courtesy" letter to let her know that the type-seven herpes virus has shown up in her blood. Make sure the letter looks official because even though there is no such thing as "type-seven herpes" who's gonna argue with a well-drafted letter from a hospital? Include information about type-seven herpes (include vague symptoms like watery eyes) and suggest treatment (such as washing the body head to toe with an anti-dandruff shampoo containing the active ingredient ketoconazole—an antifungal agent). List contact numbers for the hospital for further questions. Type her address and the hospital's address on a business envelope, stamp, and mail.

Evil Evite

TARGET: Divorced Old Guy

Set up an elaborate Evite invitation to your target's house for another friend's birthday. Send the Evite to as many people as you can. Have people call or e-mail you with questions. Tell people that food and drinks will be provided.

Don't tell **Old Guy** a thing. Once his doorbell starts ringing and doesn't stop he'll figure it out. Who knows? Maybe it will lead to an impromptu party? (Or charges and jail time.)

You're Invited!!!

Please come!

Are you coming?

Yes   No   Maybe

For the Birds

TARGET: The girls' dorm

Tools
Food for the birds

If your school has a large duck, goose, or pigeon population, see if you can use food to lure a few into the lobby of the girl's dorm. Getting them out is the hard part, and by then you will be laughing your ass off in the guy's dorm across campus.

CYA

Try to pick an early morning before people are awake and run like hell if you see anyone coming. Oh, and wear a ski mask.

Prank Pitfall

This one comes up a lot, but you can get arrested for vandalism for a prank like this. And if it's broad daylight, you might be easy to catch.

Dead Weight

TARGET: Always Raises Her Hand
Accomplices: People need to spot you on this one so recruit some strong friends

Tools

Mountain climbing rope, carabiners, and other standard rappelling gear

Whenever you rappel, you need to feel like you can trust whatever anchor from which you are rappelling *with your life*. That is why this prank is for juniors. If you are a freshman checking out the junior pranks, go back. Now, once you feel good and smart about how you are going to be suspended from the side of the building, lower yourself carefully to your target's window.

Hang upside down and put a glazed look in your eyes as if you are dead. Chances are you will scare the pants off sweet little Miss **Always**.

Prank Pitfall

If you do scare her "pants off" you might get a Peeping Tom rep. That's not cool. There's also the falling to a bloody death thing.

Sippy Cups

TARGET: The cafeteria

Accomplice: Someone who works in the cafeteria

Tools

Saran Wrap

Steal a tray of glasses from the cafeteria with the aid of your accomplice. Carefully cover the mouths of the glasses with tightly stretched Saran Wrap. Have your accomplice replace the tray with the wrapped glasses. Then step back and watch as students make a mess pouring milk, OJ, or ice onto the invisible plastic.

Or do the no-mess version: Fill the glasses with water, cranberry juice, milk, and orange juice first, then cover them with Saran Wrap. When your accomplice sets them out and students try to drink from them, it is a very funny sight.

A Rabbit Out of a Hat

TARGET: President PompAss

Tools

An unsuspecting bunny

Rabbits are quiet, cute, and inexpensive. They also shit a lot of brown pellets and eat paper. So wouldn't it be funny if one day you slipped one in through the **President**'s open window? After all, it's springtime, and what better symbol of spring than a sweet little bunny?

Tip: If you get the rabbit into the office when your target is out, it will give the rabbit a little shitting and shredding head start.

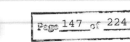

Test Time

TARGET: Smokes His Breakfast

One early Saturday morning after a vicious Friday night, wake *le target* and tell him that some girl called from his Drugs and Behavior class to remind him that they have a huge test that morning. You totally forgot to tell him. On the off chance he asks you about the day of the week or the fact that he'd never sign up for a class before 9 A.M., tell him it was a rescheduled test because the professor was out of town or something.

Prank Pitfall

*If **Smokes** is on his game that morning, he might call around to double-check, so try to sound believable so he'll fall for it. If he skips as many classes as I imagine he does, he will be an easy mark to convince.*

You Can't Judge a Book

TARGET: Pasty Library Geek

One bored afternoon, head into the book stacks and go straight to the section on "Animals of Australia" since your target's thesis topic is Tasmanian devils. Take all the books that deal with this topic and carefully remove the covers of the books. Swap around with different covers from other books. Even use books from other parts of the library; like the book on medical marvels can have the cover about zany marsupials. If that doesn't make **Pasty** turn even pastier, nothing will.

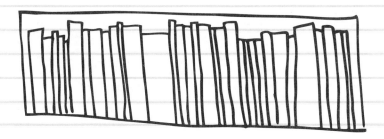

Accidents Happen

TARGET: A person in white pants

Tools

Ketchup or A1 Steak Sauce

The next time you are riding the campus shuttle and a target gets on wearing white pants, come prepared with a little bit of ketchup or A1 Steak Sauce. Offer the person your seat, but as you rise, place a dollop of the offensive condiment on the seat. When they rise they will never know about the stain on their butt; that is, until one of the lunch ladies calls them out on it.

Roach Motel

TARGET: Do-Gooding Hippie

Tools

A handful of dead cockroaches, preferably the big kind that fly

Place a handful of dead cockroaches in your target's bed while she is out. Lay a sign on her bed reading "Roach Motel." Chances are she will just pull the sign off the bed without much thought and crawl into it. When she feels the strange creatures around her feet and legs she will pull the sheets back to look. Those enormous ancient monsters are enough to freak out even the most nature-loving among us.

Push Your Luck: Don't kill the cockroaches before sticking them in her bed.

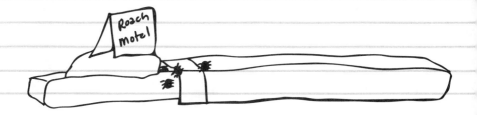

Tuna Trash

TARGET: President PompAss

Tools

Tuna and salmon water drained from cans

leave in RM (handwritten)

The next time your target makes some lame proclamation prohibiting anime heroines on T-shirts, sneak into his office when he is out of town for a week and throw into his garbage two cans' worth of tuna and salmon oil or water drained from the cans. The smell they will leave in the office will last long after the garbage has been taken out.

Vinnys Car (handwritten)

SALMON

CYA

By volunteering in the **President**'s office you will have all kinds of access to the man and his garbage. Plus, volunteering always looks good to the judge.

TUNA

Snake Pit

TARGET: Graveyard Goth

Tools

Rubber snakes and a strobe light

One night after the weirdo, I mean target, has fallen asleep with a little blood on the corner of her mouth, spread a bunch of rubber lifelike snakes all over her floor. Turn on the strobe light and blast her Marilyn Manson CD. Throw a few snakes at her as she wakes up, and watch her panic as she leaps out of bed and into the snake pit.

Prank Pitfall

She might seriously have a heart attack and die.

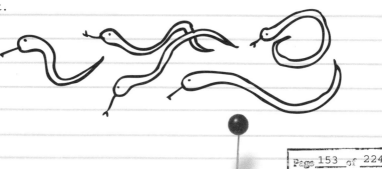

Toilet Foam

TARGET: The boys

Craigs
RM

Put a few cups of laundry detergent in the toilet tank in the boy's bathroom—not the bowl. When the unsuspecting target flushes, the soap will bubble over the brim of the toilet bowl and all over the floor. The best thing about boys is that their instinct will be to try to fix it by stopping the water from running in the bowl, but because it is foamy soap, it will probably pour over anyway and they will still be standing there in their new kicks trying in vain to stop it.

(Note, the sudsier the soap, the better.)

Neutered Mice

TARGET: Always Raises Her Hand

Your target has a huge paper due. Go into her room during a coffee break and steal the ball out of her mouse so that it won't work. If she uses a mouse with an optical sensor, tape over it. Watch her freak out over her "broken" mouse and curse modern technology. When her tech-savvy friend who is in love with her comes to help, he will have a hard time not laughing as he pulls the tape off.

Dead Coffee

TARGET: Everyone

Allison

This prank is actually really, really cruel. Crueler than flashing an old lady driving on the highway. Crueler than leading a blind person to the wrong side of the street. Well, maybe not *that* cruel. But it sucks. That's why it's in the junior section. Even though it's easy, it's so mean the level increased.

During finals, brew decaffeinated coffee and put it in the caffeinated coffee carafe. That's it. Don't tell anyone and keep doing it for as long as it amuses you, you sick, sick person.

Prank Pitfall

You will burn in hell.

Screen Changers

TARGET: Never Drinks Water

Your target has a big paper due. Get him back for passing out during your make-out session by changing the screen orientation on his computer so everything is listed sideways or upside down. You can also spice up the prank by changing his font to something girly and his background to bright pinks and yellows. Spring colors. Enlarge the font as well. And make his screen saver a bunny or a baby chick. Better yet, make it Scott Baio circa 1985 or Mr. Big.

Wall-Valanche

TARGET: Anal RA

Tools

Newspaper, duct tape, sticks, paper, and other shit (bricks optional)

The next time you find your target firmly up your ass, get him back. When he's sleeping, place newspaper across his doorframe and duct tape it, leaving a space open at the top. Then, add leaves and sticks, empty aluminum cans, or balls of paper to the space between the paper and the door so that when he opens it a mess will fall on him. Then he will be confronted by a newspaper wall!

Push Your Luck: Do the same thing but build an actual wall out of bricks or books or whatever you have handy. This will make escape more difficult and the overall prank just plain better.

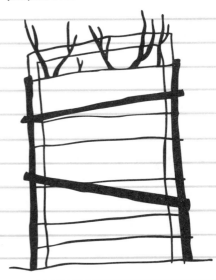

You Have Rabies

TARGET: Pasty Library Geek

Tools
A phone

Call your target and tell her that you are with the Student Health Services. Apologize for calling with this difficult news but **Pasty,** like several other members of the student body has contracted gout. Any other ancient or random illnesses are also funny and include hoof and mouth, the bubonic plague, and seborrheic dermatitis (flaky skin). You can call her more than once. It seriously never gets old.

Free Stuff

TARGET: Euro-Trash

Post an ad on Craigslist announcing that you (posing as your target) must leave the country due to a misfiling of your student visa papers. You must clean out your room ASAP. Everything must go. Then put up **Euro**'s apartment address. Go over to "hang out" and watch the drama ensue as people start showing up to take his stuff away!

Street Walkers

TARGET: The townies

This prank only works if you can rally a lot of people and if your campus has two buildings across a somewhat busy street from each other that are also connected by an underground tunnel. Get everyone to walk spread out so that there is a constant stream of people crossing the street. Continue to cross for fifteen minutes. Get this one on film. It's funny.

TARGETS: Limited Foresight and Will Do Anything to Get Some

Tools
String

This prank is for two people with rooms across from each other in the hallway of the dorm and only works with doors that open inward.

Tie a piece of string to each handle so that it is taut. Knock on both doors at the same time. When each target tries to open his door he will be struggling against the other and ostensibly locked in. The struggle is fun to watch.

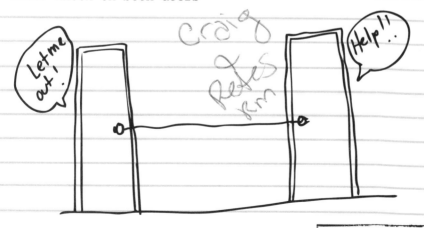

...onuts
...es His Breakfast

...ar Fred the Baker,

When **Smokes His Breakfast** came to me asking for this letter of recommendation, I have to admit I was not wholly surprised. You see, mine is the only class the young man ever attended in his eight years at this school. I teach Rastafarian Studies, an elective class offered once a week at 4:20 P.M. The class is broken down into three parts: Jamaica; Haile Selassie, Bob Marley, and Jah; and Cartoon Network. I have to admit, Mr. His Breakfast is my prized student. With straight A's and perfect attendance, it never bothered me that he took the class several times. I always appreciated how he never failed to laugh at my jokes and sell me the kindest, sweetest . . . *oregano* . . . I have ever . . . *used in spaghetti*.

Perhaps you are wondering, if this promising young man only came to one class in his college career, how could I possibly recommend him to wake up early and help you make the donuts day after day? Well, I have firsthand knowledge of **Smokes**'s baking skills, and they are truly unparalleled. Perhaps the chocolate brownies he makes have a bit of a strange flavor, but there is nothing like popping two, turning on the Wailers and busting open an icy can of brew. Nothing.

Please understand that even though the degree he finally got was more *symbolic* than, say *real*, this is a fellow who would be a perfect fit at your mall storefront. I certainly hope you will consider him for the position.

With one love and one heart,

Professor Buttons Unbuttoned

Professor Buttons Unbuttoned

Senior Pranks

Pranks for Peeps Who Have Friends on the Campus Police Squad (and a Few Faculty Allies)

Now it's time for the big guns. After all, you are bigger than everyone else on campus and can probably run faster. You are ogling the fresh meat and ready to take on the next phase of your life. I'd say you're as bored as hell if you didn't already say it with your eyes the minute you picked up this book! So go ahead and throw away the whoopee cushions and the cream pies. It's time to swap the orientation video on date rape with the hardcore porn. You're a senior now. You're done with the kid stuff.

Crime of Passion

TARGET: Pasty Library Geek

Accomplice: A victim

Tools

Fake blood, a bloody piece of T-shirt

Begin this fight near where **Pasty** is studying late one weekend night far from library staff. In fact, stage the fight within five feet of her so she is sure to hear even though you are limited to a library whisper. Ideally, set the fight between two men, as it will really scare her. Allow it to escalate. Include a single staged punch (or real if you or your accomplice are prepared to take it like a man). Now, step away from the sufficiently terrified girl. The next time she gets up to go into the book stacks begin the fight in earnest. Really "pummel" each other, so as she peers through the stacks she will think she is witnessing a violent

attack. Have one of you begin pleading for your life desperately. Pretty soon **Pasty** will run off to find help. Now set up the scene of the crime with your bloody piece of cloth and some blood that appears to have been dragged down the aisle.

CYA

Hide out in a bathroom at the far end of the library for five minutes, then run like hell out of there.

Ball Players

TARGET: The basketball team

Accomplices: Enough guys to make up a basketball team

Tools

Basketball uniforms from a random team

Put on uniforms from a random school and show up at a basketball game. When they call out the opposing team, come out with *your* team as well. Look at the confused players like you are also confused. Explain that you thought your team, the Gerbils, was supposed to be playing that day. Challenge the opposing team to a shoot-out to pick who plays. Act pissed off and storm out if you are denied the chance to play.

Nonprofit Antics

TARGET: Do-Gooding Hippie

Accomplice: Minimum three—one to make the speech, one to hand out fliers, and one to arrive with the target and egg her on as a fellow protester; but as many people as you can rally so you look more authentic

Tools

Signs, professional looking pamphlets, posters of starving children with red Xs across their pathetic mugs

Set up a booth somewhere on campus to hand out false literature promoting a new organization: Young, White, Catholic Republicans for World Peace Through Fire Power and Financial Sanctions, or the YWCR. Get a group of friends to act as photographers and supporters. Make signs and fliers. Make sure the head of the organization has a soapbox and a microphone. Have him or her espouse all the virtues of the group—talk about peace through domination, plans to brow-beat a little sense into those heathens, and don't forget, bandy the word "commie" as much as possible.

Make sure **Do-Gooding Hippie** arrives with an accomplice who can help instigate a confrontation between her and the YWCR. Watch as **Do-Gooding**'s face goes from red to purple in her vain efforts to be heard. Let the YWCR's antics escalate. Make mention of giving all foreign assholes, insurgents, and people with a contrary opinion a puppy and if they can keep it alive for a month, they will get a fair trial. But if the puppy dies, they will get a bullet between the eyes.

Keep it up until dinner or until the hippie throws a punch—or wait until the real media arrives. If it gets on TV, you are a badass.

Prank Pitfall

You become known as the KKK Red Dragon of the school.

Athletic Wars

TARGET: The jocks

Tools

Silverware, balloons, beach balls, feathers, grease

Freeze silverware from the cafeteria into the school hockey rink. Fill the top of the campus pool with as many balloons, beach balls, or feathers as you can gather. Grease the gymnastics equipment. Steal the basketball nets.

And finally, topple the goalposts on the football field. You might need accomplices if you do it all at once. If you spread the pranks out over a few weeks, you might be able to pull them off yourself.

The Land of Dixie

TARGET: Creepy and Antisocial

Tools

Many Dixie cups and a stapler

Go into your target's room when he is out for a while. Carefully create a grid of Dixie cups by stapling the top of the lips together. As you go, fill the rows of cups with water. Once you get to the door, you should be standing before a grid of Dixie cups covering the floor, each full of water. When **Creepy** returns to his room, he will not know how to begin to take apart your masterful work. But it will be loads of fun watching him try!

It's even more fun if you set up the grid while your target sleeps. It's also more dangerous.

Bail-Out Plan

TARGET: President PompAss

Using realistic letter-head from the law firm of Sewickly, Benedict, and Sewickly, send out a letter informing your target that a donation in excess of $10 million has been endowed to Hellshire University by a recently deceased alumnus. (Look at a copy of the latest alumni magazine in the library for names of the recently deceased.) Rules for the money include: $2 million toward an undergraduate scholarship fund, $5 million toward faculty housing, and the rest for general campus expenses. Have one stipulation: Students and faculty must be allowed to vote every four years on who should be university president.

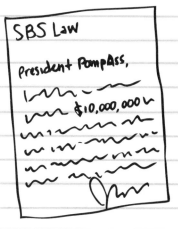

SBS Law

President PompAss,

$10,000,000

Prank Pitfall

The guy might hate his job enough to agree to the stipulation.

Picture Perfect

TARGET: Alterna-Chick

Tools

A darkroom, a film camera, and a roll of film

This prank requires a little sleight of hand. For anyone who has ever taken a photography class, you know that you are encouraged to begin by developing a contact sheet on which all of your negatives are exposed as small pictures. In order to make a contact sheet, **Alterna** must cut her negatives and slip them into sleeves, then expose them on an enlarger and put them into the developing solution. My suggestion is to swap **Alterna**'s negatives with your own negatives while the negatives are drying—before she cuts them. Then when she makes her contact sheet, all the pictures on your rolls will appear instead of her own. So think of your roll of film as telling a story. Perhaps shoot pictures of a staged kidnapping. Or her boyfriend or the boyfriend of her friend having a (fake) affair. But be creative. And don't do anything that offends women, children, or small animals. Thank you.

Having **Alterna-Chick** develop an unexpected image is harder to pull off and may require even more forethought. First of all, be "working" next to her in the darkroom. Once she has chosen her image she must expose it using an enlarger before she develops it. Somehow, get her attention for long enough that you switch the image she just exposed on developing paper with the one you made for her. Then when she lays it down into the solution to watch her image appear, instead of the crocus cluster she was expecting, up will come a picture of a man's deep-set eyes staring her down beside a sign in the back reading, "I'm watching you." If that's too scary, you can just have her develop a person's face with their tongue sticking out. Or whatever. Come up with your own zany idea. Again, do nothing to anything that cannot or will not consent.

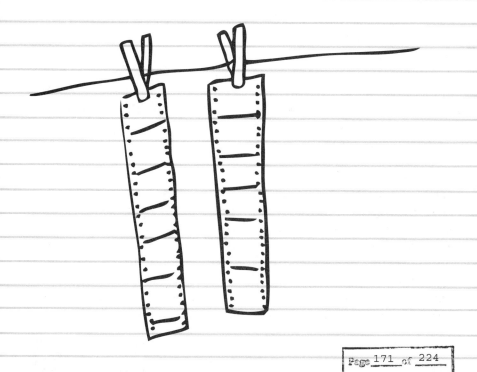

Law Un-Enforcement

TARGET: Your parents and President PompAss

Send a letter home to your parents on university letterhead explaining that Hellshire University regrets to inform them that it can no longer be held accountable for minors drinking alcohol on campus. The costs of enforcing the current national law has become far too prohibitive for the university to uphold. Therefore any events being held on campus will no longer be policed in the same way they once were. If alcohol is sold at any events, IDs will not be checked. The Greek houses will have to protect themselves from underage drinking by hiring their own security.

The responsibility of checking IDs and enforcing the law will be left to the student organizers. On the upside, the university feels certain that this student body was raised right and will do the right thing. Sign the letter with the forged signature of **President PompAss**.

Flying Ford

TARGET: Everyone

Accomplices: A dorky engineer and a car geek

Tools

Old car parts or a junker

This prank is a toughie, but definitely possible and ultimately worth the effort. Begin by gathering car parts from a junkyard, or if you know a car ready to be junked, even better! The car can be brought up to the roof of a dorm or campus center in pieces. Once all the parts are up there, reassemble it. You have until sunrise. The good news is that it doesn't have to run, so the engine (one of the heaviest parts) does not have to get onto the roof. In the morning, everyone will wonder how a car flew to the top of a building.

Then they will wonder how to get it down. But first they will laugh.

Push Your Luck: Create a pulley system and actually hoist the car of an administrator, faculty member, or annoying fellow student to the roof. This requires an evil mastermind.

Prank Pitfall

You could fall off the roof and die if you are not careful. So could the car.

Lights Out

TARGET: Always Raises Her Hand

Tools

Black lights, painting supplies, and invisible neon paint

Set up a series of black lights in the dorm. The plug-in socket type is a great way to pull this off. Paint the walls with invisible neon paint. You and an accomplice should plug in all the black lights. When you turn off all the lights in the hall, have your accomplice turn on the black lights. Make sure your messages are creepy, funny, or flat-out terrifying. If your target doesn't have a heart attack, your RA probably will.

CYA

Act as freaked out as everybody else and you should blend in nicely.

GET ME OUT OF HERE! HELP!

Ghost in the Classroom

TARGET: Professor Gasbag

Tools

Ouija board and a story about ghosts

Turn in a short story for your next creative writing class about Ouija boards and ghosts. Bring in a Ouija board to class the day of your critique as a sort of "visual aid." Whether or not you get the class to play with it, it is just enough to elevate the ghostly tension. The next day, arrive to class before anyone gets there and stack the chairs. Ideally, find an impossible way to stack using fishing line. A single levitating chair will make a bold impression. Leave and come back to the room at the same time as the rest of the class. Whisper loudly, "It must have been the Ouija board." If everyone is very quiet, scream.

Drop Trou

TARGET: The whole campus
Accomplices: About fifty

This prank is best set for between classes when a lot of people are walking across the quad. Choose a specific time to have about fifty people agree to be a part of this prank. On their way to class, at exactly five minutes to eleven, they should take off their pants and continue walking. After two minutes they should put their pants back on and keep going on as if nothing happened.

Rock Band

TARGET: Pasty Library Geek

Accomplices: Three friends with instruments and a few people to act as "groupies"

Tools

Amps, speakers, and instruments

Set up a band outside the library. Play as horribly as you can while still looking earnest. Plant a few die-hard groupies who are totally grooving to your tunes. When your target or members of the faculty try to get you to turn it down, have your fans start screaming about freedom of expression and how this school is choking your creativity. When they unplug you, cry.

Prank Pitfall

Depending on how far you take this, if the real cops get involved instead of the campus cops you could wind up doing time. That's your first warning.

Chicken Little

TARGET: Greek Asshole

Tools

Live chickens, chicken feed

Live grown chickens are fairly easy to buy and are surprisingly inexpensive; $5–$10 will usually buy one. Look up hatcheries in your area. Once you have procured a few feathered friends, break into the frat house and, on top of a large pile of chicken feed, release the chickens. Not only is getting them out of the house a challenge, but the smell will never be forgotten.

Prank Pitfall

Getting the chickens to the frat house could be a challenge. The smell is bad. Really, really bad. Also, any killing of chickens, accidental or otherwise is wrong. Really, really wrong.

Stolen Street Signs

TARGET: Campus Po-Po

Accomplices: Ten to twenty people good at stealing shit

Tools

Legally procured street sign or similar item

Buy a large street sign, stop sign, traffic light, or other similar item at an antique or novelty store. Later, walk around campus carrying it proudly. When the campus police stop you to ask about it, show them your receipt then explain that you keep getting stopped. Ask if they can just tell the rest of the campus cops that you are legally carrying the item and to leave you alone. After he radios that there is a kid carrying a sign he bought and to just ignore it, have your accomplices begin stealing signs and walking home with them.

Push Your Luck: If you are in a small town, even better is if you can get the local cops to radio that you are on the up and up. You can get a lot better loot that way.

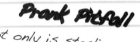

Prank Pitfall

Not only is stealing wrong, it is punishable. Just saying.

Roof Room

TARGET: Graveyard Goth

One of these days, all that maudlin mood music is really going to take its toll. One night, when **Graveyard** is staying at her even weirder and abundantly pierced boyfriend's house, move her bedroom piece by piece to the roof of the dorm. Set it up exactly as she had it set up, with her medieval skeleton collection beside her bed and the formaldehyde finger on the dresser. Use a clothesline or rolling rack to simulate her closet and hang her clothes. Keep the rest of her clothes in dressers.

Prank Pitfall

If it rains or the elements otherwise wreak destruction upon her items, the prank goes from funny to criminal. Check the weather.

Toilet Hall

TARGET: Anal RA

Tools

Power tools

One night when everyone is sleeping, dismantle a toilet from the dorm bathroom. This can be done with some simple power tools. Just remember to turn off the water first. Set the toilet outside your target's door. Place a single bathroom stall around it setting it up so the door meets up flush with **Anal**'s room. Once your stall has been totally set up, complete with a roll of toilet paper in the dispenser, knock. Then hide.

Inmate/Outmate

TARGET: Do-Gooding Hippie

Post an announcement on a campus bulletin board requesting buddies for an outpatient program coordinated by a nearby mental hospital through the university, asking students to host inmates in need of special assistance. The student will be asked to spend one day a week with the inmate, allowing them to shadow them to their classes and meals. The student will be asked to tutor them and help them catch up on work they missed. The idea is to inspire a love of learning in the individual in the hopes that it will aid in their healing.

When **Do-Gooding** signs up, send her out a thick folder of information about her inmate. All the information should indicate that this is one sick individual, and potentially dangerous. Send away for information from rehab facilities and write notes as if you are a doctor of psychology or a psychiatrist or both. List medication the individual is taking, including drugs for schizophrenia, Tourette's syndrome, bipolar disorder, and methadone for heroin withdrawal. As a final touch, include a handwritten note from the creepy inmate telling **Do-Gooding** how much he is looking forward to spending time with her. The thicker you lay it on, the better.

Prank Pitfall

Avoid rape or murder threats. It's funny enough if she just thinks the guy is going to start yelling the words "ass muncher" during her biology class. If you start threatening intense bodily harm to people, not only do you start to look like a supreme asshole, but you begin flirting with a lawsuit.

Hose Stopper

TARGET: Always Raises Her Hand

Tools
A hose

When your target starts the new garden this spring, pull up a hose and tie it off in the center so that the water gets stopped. Next, go to **Always** and looking into the nozzle, tell her you think you see something. As she looks into the end of the hose, release the knot. If you are wondering why this is a senior prank it is because you will have to run like hell to get away from your pissed-off target. The thing about her is that she does not hit like a girl.

Forks

TARGET: The campus cleaning crew
Accomplices: Two to ten friends

Tools

Many metal forks and Vaseline

Over a few months, steal forks from the dining hall. One night, divide the quad into sections among you and your accomplices. Grease the end of the forks with the Vaseline and start sticking the pronged ends into the grass of the quad. Place them about a foot apart covering every inch of grass. When the university goes to clean up the mess you made, the Vaseline will make pulling the forks out of the ground virtually impossible. But it will be fun to watch them trying!

CYA

Tell them it was an art installation and your professor made you do it. If they ask which professor, point at the sky, yell "What's *that*?" and run like hell.

Prank Pitfall

If you get caught, it will be you pulling the greased forks out of the ground.

Short Sheeting

TARGET: Greek Asshole

This joke has been around since our grandparents were our age. But it never gets old. Very simply, take **Greek**'s sheets, both bottom and top, and fold them about one-third of the way up. Tuck them in around the sides so it stays that way. Cover it all up with a blanket. When **Greek** crawls into bed, nothing will seem out of place until he slides his feet into the folded sheet and can't go down any further. It's never dull to watch someone struggle to spread the sheet back out and down.

Prank Pitfall

He might punch you. But it'll still be worth it.

Skeleton Crew

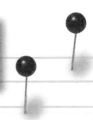

TARGET: Pasty Library Geek

Accomplice: A person to signal you to move the skeleton and also videotape the reaction for posterity

Steal "Mortimer" the human skeleton from the bio lab. Set him up in the hallway and connect fishing line to his legs and arms. Hide out. (One possibility is to stand outside a window and run the line inside to the hallway but any way you can conceal yourself will work!) Next, wait for your target, or anyone else for that matter, to walk by. Have an accomplice signal you (or use your ears) and begin moving the skeleton's limbs wildly. I bet you your target will drop her coffee, books, and probably a load.

Push Your Luck: Create a penile bone to attach at the pelvis. When your target walks by, give Mortimer a "boner." Or, use a microphone and a small strategically placed speaker so that you can have Morty say hello.

Iambic Pentameter

TARGET: Professor Buttons Unbuttoned

Call your professor posing as a highbrow magazine like *Harper's* or the *New Yorker* and ask her for an article on academic life written in iambic pentameter. Have her e-mail it to an address you set up—tell her that you are having her use your personal address because the system at the magazine keeps shutting down, or claim to be a freelance editor calling on behalf of the magazine. Give her a forty-eight-hour deadline explaining that the issue, focusing on academics in America, is going to print at the end of the week.

Whatever she sends, print, Xerox, and paper the school with it. Or just do a schoolwide e-mail blast if you want to save the trees. But her wasted time might be reward enough without adding humiliation to it.

Laugh with the Sinners

TARGET: Smokes His Breakfast

Accomplices: The whole floor of the dorm

Tools

Dry ice, fan, spot light, battery-powered mic and speakers

This prank takes some serious setup, but is well worth the effort. Remember when **Smokes** quit smoking and became a holy roller? During those rants about the greatness of God and the impending Armageddon, he was sure to let all of you know that *you* were going to be left with the sinners while *he* got to go to salvation. This prank gives you the chance to get him back. (Note: It works best if you get the target high, so try to talk him into a one-time smoke or hope he's already killed a sufficient number of brain cells.) Fill the floor of the hall with dry ice. Using a fan, spread the steam out. Trip the fuse box so all the electricity goes out in the building. Flash a single spot light in through a hall window from a neighboring building. Using a battery-powered microphone connected to several battery-powered speakers, send God's voice out to your target: "You have sinned and shall remain on Earth. Only the godly will be saved."

When the lights come back on and the smoke clears, **Smokes** will have to accept that he's been left with the sinners. May as well smoke 'em if you got 'em!

Looking for Love

TARGET: Backwards Baseball Cap

Tools
Tape, a Sharpie, and a piece of paper

For this prank you can be creative and come up with any sign you wish, but I recommend the classic: "I desperately want to make love to a schoolboy" taped to the passenger-side window of your target's car. Because that's just funny.

Prank Pitfall

People are homophobic and crazy. You don't want to subject your friend to the insanity of the public, and sending him to drive in a car basically claiming that he's a pedophile is not a way to avoid that possible end.

I DESPERATELY WANT TO MAKE LOVE TO A SCHOOLBOY.

Men Working

TARGET: People with cars

Accomplices: Burly worker types

Tools

Hard hats, a jackhammer, cones, tape and protective clothes, a white work truck, and eyewear

Dress up as a worker and cordon off an area of road that goes through the heart of campus. Dig up a big hole or two through the pavement and leave. Chances are no one will notice for a while unless they are driving.

Push Your Luck: Do this trick a second time if no one calls this out as a prank. The next time real workers are digging anywhere close to campus, chances are the cops will stop them in their tracks assuming it's a bunch of pranksters.

Sign Swap

TARGET: Only Speaks Football and the rest of the fans
Accomplice: Someone on the cheer squad

This is a classic from the Rose Bowl in 1961 when the Minnesota Golden Gophers played the Washington Huskies. A third school stole the show by getting its name on TV when flip cards in the stands revealed the words "CAL TECH" in huge letters.

In a similar fashion, before a game swap a pile of the cheerleader's cards with the words "GO HELLSHIRE" on them with ones that read "GO SOME OTHER TEAM!"

Another one to try: If you can get enough people to do it, show up at a game dressed as fans of a third, random school. It will be funny *and* confusing.

School Closing

TARGET: Your parents

Send out a memo/e-mail from the dean of students to all the students and their parents saying that the school has run out of money and will not be opening its doors for the subsequent school year in order to restructure. Students going abroad or taking the year off will not be affected. However, students registered to come back will not be refunded but will be invited back the following year at an adjusted rate. If the student decides to take the year at another school they will be given the option to return to Hellshire in the appropriate class.

> **Tip:** Keep your language and your materials believable by using university letterhead for the letter itself as well as the envelope. Type the addresses instead of writing them by hand.

About Face

TARGET: Pasty Library Geek

Accomplices: Hearty engineering types

Tools

Flashlights, shovels, building materials to construct the A-frame and pulley system

You know that bronze statue that faces the library? Your target finds it very comforting, like a friendly face bidding her goodnight at the end of each long study session. For this prank, a lot of preparation is needed. First, investigate. Turn off or limit the vision of nearby security cameras. On the night of the prank, turn off the lights in the area and use flashlights. Dig around the statue to loosen its base. Build an A-frame with pulleys and hoist the statue up. Then turn it around to have it face the other direction. The next day when **Pasty** finds herself *greeted* by the statue, she won't know what happened.

Note, if the statue just won't budge, you can always just give it a jaunty hat and feathered boa and see how that strikes Pasty.

Prank Pitfall

There might be damage to the statue if you aren't careful and don't know what you're doing.

Will You Marry Me?

TARGET: Only Speaks Football
Accomplice: The guy who programs the stuff on the Jumbotron and the target's girlfriend

Tools

Tickets to a big game

Offer your target two tickets for your target and his lady to go to the big game on their anniversary. When they are in the stands, have the Jumbotron read, "Girlfriend, will you marry me? Love, **Only Speaks Football**." Now, have the girlfriend get all excited, shouting, *"Yes!"* and jumping up and down. When **Only Speaks Football** tries letting her know he didn't have anything to do with the sign, have her haul off and slap him.

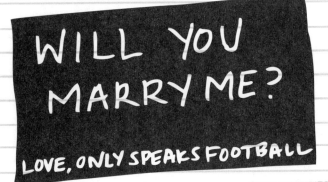

WILL YOU MARRY ME?
LOVE, ONLY SPEAKS FOOTBALL

Teepee Village

TARGET: Everyone

Accomplices: People who can help you build things

Tools

Fabric, rope, paint, and wood poles

Teepees are fairly easy structures to build and require few tools. You can find out how to build them online. Set up a realistic teepee village on the residential quad, so when students wake up and come outside they will see a series of teepees there with no rhyme or reason.

Push Your Luck: Add chickens, a cow or two, and a horse to the scene.

Push Your Luck Even More: Have people dress up in Native American attire and go about their business as though they are supposed to be there. You might even trick the school into thinking this is a legit, albeit hilarious, class project.

Feminist Outrage

TARGET: Greek Asshole

Find out when the next obnoxious frat party involving wet T-shirts is taking place. You and a group of girlfriends should enter the contest. Write feminist slogans all over your bodies. When you stand up in your wet T-shirt, your messages will be revealed. This prank might not really make your point as well as you'd hoped, but I guarantee no one loses where wet T-shirts are concerned, feminist slogans or not.

Push Your Luck: If you actually want to freak these guys out and do a little permanent damage, enter the contest with freakishly long underarm hair (add it cosmetically if your pits are smooth as a baby's bottom) then in unison, just after your shirt has been rendered invisible, raise those arms up high and proud!

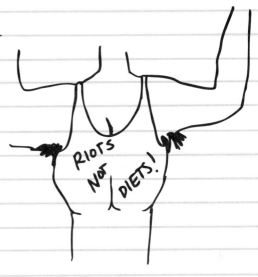

Surprise Dinner Guest

TARGET: Do-Gooding Hippie
Accomplice: The head

Tools

Covers for dinner plates and a table with a hole in it big enough for a human head to fit through, a tablecloth

So you know how your target finally decided to give up meat? Invite her over for a vegetarian dinner party. Greet your guests explaining that you have worked really hard on this dinner, your first attempt to cook without meat. Have everyone say grace holding hands. Say one, two, three, and have them all lift up their plate covers. Underneath **Do-Gooding**'s will be a surprise head who has been waiting under the table beneath the plate cover. It will be the surprise of your new vegetarian's life. Afterward, go out for a pepperoni pizza.

Three-Way Calling

TARGET: Limited Foresight and President PompAss

Your two targets are sick of talking to each other since the first is always getting into trouble and the second is always dealing with it. Using a public phone with three-way calling capability, call the prez and pretend you are **Limited Foresight.** Ask him to wait a second and get **Limited** on the phone telling him you are the **President**'s secretary. Once they are connected, listen to the totally confused conversation and try not to laugh so that they can hear you.

You can use the same basic premise and connect two rival pizza places or two people who used to date.

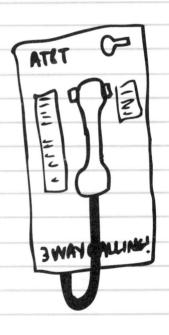

Blaze of Glory

TARGET: Divorced Old Guy

Tools

Paper bag, dog crap, matches

Your target wants you to come over and see his new disco ball in the bachelor pad. It's impolite not to bring the host a gift! Here is a classic prank reworked college style: In a paper bag put some fresh crap. Light the bag on fire and ring the doorbell. When he opens the door, **Divorced** is likely to step on the flames. Once they are out, make sure you have run to the backdoor where you will knock loudly. On his way to answer your knock he will track shit all the way through his house on the night of his big party.

When you arrive later, remark on how good everything smells. Like springtime in the country!

Prank Pitfall

Old Guy has been around the block and probably knows this prank already. Then there's also the fact that you are dealing with real fire that burns and destroys things. Make sure you have a fire extinguisher and a really good pair of running shoes, just in case.

Wear Your President to School Day

TARGET: President PompAss

Accomplices: The Whole Student Body

Tools

White T-shirts, incriminating pics of the President

Make and distribute a slew of white T-shirts with that notorious picture of the **President** falling asleep at last year's commencement ceremony. Or the one of him picking his nose during the Christmas dance pageant. Blow his huge head up even bigger and then schedule a day for everyone to come out wearing it. Tip: This prank works best on the day of some kind of an event where the target and most of his staff will see it, so plan accordingly.

Prank Pitfall

This prank costs more than others, especially because it requires a whole lot of T-shirts and a whole lot of people to wear them. Try to split the cost if you can.

Test Taking

TARGET: TA with the 'Tude

Have you pretty much had it by year four with this a-hole? It's finally time to get him back. Send an e-mail out from his account (of course you're sneaky enough to break into it, you brilliant senior, you!). Tell all 300 students in his freshman intro class that they have to pick up a take-home quiz worth half their grade by the next afternoon. Tell them that they need to come by his office hours either that evening or tomorrow morning (best is to use his real office hours so that he will be there) and let them know he will instruct them on what is expected. When his office hours get flooded with students freaking out and asking for their tests he won't have any idea what they're talking about. But it will still be funny.

National Monument

TARGET: The whole school

Accomplices: Builders, art students, and volunteers

Tools

Hammer and nails, building materials, paints, and a location to build it, also a trailer or truck to transport

This prank is hilarious but requires a ton of prep work, a lot of elbow grease, and some measure of talent. Think you have what it takes? Then by all means, construct and transport to your campus a life-size Statue of Liberty torch and head to have it coming out of the snow like the kids at the University of Wisconsin did in the 1970s. The Liberty Bell in the dining hall will also work or some other unmistakable national monument in the middle of the quad. No one will believe their eyes when they go

outside and see the Holly-
wood sign standing proudly
on the nearby hills of
Hellshire. They will be
stunned and amazed when a
replica space shuttle ap-
pears on the campus lawn
or when the Rocky statue

shows up in the middle of
the swimming pool.

Tip: This prank works
best if the monument is
revealed overnight in one
fell swoop rather than
piecemeal.

Tucked In

TARGET: Smokes His Breakfast

Tools

Saran Wrap

One night after your tar-
get is mindblown and
passed out, sneak into his
room and carefully wrap
him and the bed in Sa-
ran Wrap. Work quickly and
carefully going over him
and under the bed until
he is Saran-Wrapped to it.
Leave him under his blan-
ket and don't wrap him too
tightly or he will wake

up. In the morning he will
have no idea what happened
and will have quite a time
getting out of the invis-
ible straitjacket you cre-
ated for him.

Fly Pizza

TARGET: Backwards Baseball Cap

Tools

Plastic bugs

You know how your target will only ever eat the pizza in the dining hall? Shove a few plastic bugs under the mushrooms or pepperoni or underneath some bubbly cheese. When he starts eating and gets to the bug he will wish he had a more sophisticated palate. Throw one in his drink for good measure when he's not looking so when he goes to wash the nasty pizza down he follows it up with a rubber bug in his Coke.

Prank Pitfall

Others will inevitably get bugs from the other slices you contaminated. But that's still funny. Then there's also the possibility of someone choking on a fake spider or someone puking on you.

Water Tower Monster

TARGET: The townies

Accomplice: Limited Foresight

Tools

Your favorite art supplies, ski masks (optional)

Want to bring the whole town into a prank? Decorate your water tower! Turn him into a big scary monster with teeth and purple fur. Do it overnight so that in the morning the town wakes up to their own personal Godzilla.

CYA

Wear ski masks if the tower has cameras, work quickly and then get the hell out of there.

University for Sale

TARGET: President PompAss

Take out an ad in the paper announcing that a large home with ample kitchen space, guest quarters, an efficient staff, a private gym, and an indoor pool is available for immediate purchase. End the ad with, "Comes with 5,000 residents."

Push Your Luck: Hang an enormous FOR SALE sign (five stories or more) over the most visible academic or residential hall, in huge, red block letters.

Remote Control

TARGET: Anyone

Tools

Universal remote

Use a universal remote
control and set it to work
with the television in the
student lounge, the fac-
ulty lounge, or on the
Campus Center TVs. If your
remote has a good long-
range signal, you can
change the channels from
another room. But even if
it doesn't, it's fun to sit
at a table and use those
buttons underneath it,
fighting over the big game
and *Semi-Homemade with
Sandra Lee*. Or porn.

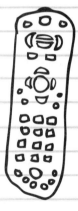

Fame

TARGET: Everyone

Plan this one out carefully. Get a large group of people to choreograph a dance to *Fame* by Irene Cara. Then, using the sound system at the campus center with additional speakers snuck in and strategically placed, one day during a busy time start playing the song. Have everyone look around at everyone else in confusion. Then have a few people just break into a perfectly coordinated dance routine. As the song goes on, have more people join in adding totally synchronized or harmonious moves. Continue to build it until a lot of people are dancing a totally planned-out and synchronized dance. People will have no idea what's going on, but they will have a really good time watching you.

Tip: Videotape this one from several angles for sure.

Cue Ball

TARGET: Euro-Trash

Tools

Sharp hair scissors

Are you flat-out tired of your buddy **Euro-Trash** and his obsession with the oil slick he calls a ponytail running down his back? Are you done with the smell of shoe polish in your car? This prank is the prank for you.

First, take your boy out for one last greasy hurrah to the club of his choice. Buy him a few extra shots. Then take him home to sleep it off. Once he's passed out, carefully snip that pony tail and as many hairs as possible around it. The sharper the scissors, the easier the cutting and, thus, the less likely to wake him.

Push Your Luck: Shave it off, baby. Shave it off.

CYA

In the morning when he calls you mad as hell, deny everything and mention the note you saw on his desk when you dropped him off. There he will find an anonymous note from a pissed-off female claiming she is happy to finally be over him!

Breaking the Eggs

TARGET: Creepy and Antisocial

Tools
Silly Putty and string

This prank takes quite a bit of prep, but once it's in place it is a good one. Wait until your target is out squirrel shooting and you have some time for setup. Using the Silly Putty, attach the string to the Silly Putty egg. Tie the string to the metal grid part of the drop ceiling common in most dorms. (If yours doesn't have a drop ceiling, you might be able to attach the eggs to the ceiling with more Silly Putty.) Hang the eggs all over the room at shoulder level or lower so that you cannot walk anywhere without hitting one. Next, go around and put a little bit of water in each egg and carefully put it back together. Leave the egg a little loose so that it will only take a little bump to make it come apart. Work your way from the back of the room to the door. When you are done and **Creepy** comes home, he will not be able to walk without breaking the eggs and spilling water all over his room. Cleanup will be maddening.

Push Your Luck: Fill the eggs with paint (washable if you don't want to get sued for damages). Tuna juice and liquor also work and have the added benefit of stinking up the place. (Of course, that would be an awful waste of valuable liquor. . . .)

Dog Swap

TARGET: Dog owners

Tools
Dog treats (optional)

You know all those students who treat their dogs like crap but keep them anyway for status? For this prank, go around and gather up some of those abused canines by breaking into their owner's pet-friendly campus apartment. (Bring meat treats so you don't get your head bitten off.) Then swap that dog with another person's dog. If the owners even notice that their dog isn't their dog, maybe it will teach them a lesson.

Prank Pitfall

It is breaking and entering and theft to steal a dog.

"Darling Nikki" on Bells

TARGET: Everyone

You will have to do a white-collar crime in order to hack into the campus system, but if you are savvy or know the right people, you can reprogram the campus clock to chime "Darling Nikki" by Prince on the hour. Too bad you can't get it to sing those raunchy lyrics too.

Freshman Map

TARGET: All new students

Accomplice: Someone who works at the school paper

On the first day of school publish an incorrect map of campus. Make sure you put most of the buildings that freshmen frequent on the far side of campus, far away from the freshmen residence halls.

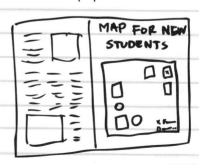

Big Winner

TARGET: Only Speaks Football
Accomplice: The game announcer and several people behind the scenes

This prank is one where it helps to know people in the athletic department. You know how most athletic events have some kind of halftime event where a student in the stands can win a car or a pile of money or a spring break trip for nailing a free throw, a field goal kick, or something similar? Well, for this prank, have the game announcer call out the seat of your target as the big winner of the grand prize. All he has to do is kick a field goal blindfolded from fifty yards away. Now, while they are ushering him onto the field, have him escorted out of the stands so that you can announce to the rest of the stadium that when he kicks, no matter where the ball goes they need to cheer their asses off like he just won the grand prize of $50,000. When **Football** shows up on the field, get him blindfolded and then let the games begin. While he is celebrating his enormous win, come out and announce that it was a prank. Heartbreaking and oh-so satisfying!

Hellshire University

To: Greenpeace
RE: Do-Gooding Hippie

Dear Cherry Idaho Sumatra,

I am writing on the "recycled paper of the spirit of the great pine of America" on behalf of **Do-Gooding Hippie**, a young lady of superior, if misguided, intentions. **Do-Gooding** has succeeded in pointing out every carbon footprint this university and everyone in it leaves on what she calls her "Mother." In fact, my office fields roughly fifteen phone calls per week from this, shall we say, persistent young lady with complaints ranging from the wasteful practice of having a campus shuttle loop to the use of "murdered" animals in our cafeterias.

    Do-Gooding is the kind of focused individual who forgoes showers in order to respect our waters, using instead buckets of runoff water from the showers of her dorm-mates that would otherwise wastefully drain. Further, she only wears used clothing mindlessly thrown out by her fellow students. She forgoes laundry entirely for patchouli incense. The nice thing about this, of course, is that one always knows she is coming and is therefore able to "be in an important meeting" when she arrives.

    She has informed me that she has in her young life saved fourteen trees, six bald eagles, and one baby seal. And even though her parents are multimillionaires who own a corporation that dumps over 800 tons of garbage per day into the Hudson River, her only personal extravagance is a set of silk sheets and biannual $180 haircuts that help shape her dreadlocks.

Regards,

President PompASS

President PompASS

Final Exam

Are you the kind of prankster that deserves a diploma from Hellshire University? If so, you will pass the following exam. Give yourself the allotted points for whichever answer most closely resembles your own.

1. Off the top of your head can you make up three pranks?

If you can't think of any: 0 points
If you can think of one: 1 pt.
If you can think of two: 2 pts.
If you can think of three: 3 pts.

2. Do you know at least three secrets about another person that you have never told another soul?

For no secrets kept: 0 pts.
For one secret kept: 1 pt.
For two secrets kept: 2 pts.
For three secrets kept: 3 pts.

3. Do you have at least three friends you can trust who would make good accomplices?

For zero trustworthy friends: 0 pts.
For one trustworthy friend: 1 pt.
For two trustworthy friends: 2 pts.
For three trustworthy friends: 3 pts.

4. Are you a patient and deliberate person?

Do you go from having the idea to executing right away? 0 pts.
Do you take a day to work out the details of a prank? 1 pt.
Do you take two days to figure out a prank? 2 pts.
Do you take three days to really figure out what you want to do? 3 pts.

5. Are you frugal?

Can you pull off a prank for under $1? 3 pts.
Can you pull off a prank for around $5? 2 pts.
Does it cost you at least $10 to pull off a prank? 1 pt.
Do you pretty much always spend more than $10 on all your pranks? 0 pts.

6. How nimble are you?

Can you pull off a prank in under a minute and get away fast? 3 pts.
Do you need five minutes to pull off a prank? 2 pts.
Do you need ten minutes to get a prank done? 1 pt.
Does it take you upwards of ten minutes to finish a prank? 0 pts.

7. How quiet are you?

Do most people say your laugh sounds like the tinkling of a bell? 3 pts.
Would you say your laugh is pretty normal? 2 pts.
Do you have a loud, boisterous laugh? 1 pt.
Have you been told your cackle resembles that of a hyena? 0 pts.

8. Do you have sadistic tendencies?

When pranking do you sometimes hope your target will feel pain? 0 pts.
During a prank do you sometimes hope you will draw blood? 1 pt.
When pranking, do you try to have some regard for the relative safety of your target? 2 pts.
During a prank is your target's physical safety of the utmost importance to you? 3 pts.

Score

Add up your score and read the following results:

19–24 Points—Graduate with Honors: Congratulations! We are proud to announce that you have passed your final with flying colors. You are officially a graduate of this fine institution. You are invited to Xerox your ass on a copier, write your name and the date under the words "Hellshire University" somewhere near the butt-crack, frame it, and hang it on your wall. You should be proud (or vaguely concerned).

13–18 Points—The Guy Who Graduates Last Is Still a Graduate: Nice one. You made it through our esteemed program. While you did not make the dean's list, you completed enough of the course work to march with the rest of your class. We recommend however, a few summer school classes to hone a few of your skills. You are a Prankster, 2nd class.

7–12 Points—See You Next Year: Close but no cigar. You will not be taking home a diploma this year. Pranking is a dangerous practice, and we'd like you to stay out of prison until after your kids move out of the house. But keep trying. If you weren't so busy messing around, you could start in on some serious messing around.

0–6 Points—Already Took Out an Eye: Step away from the rubber gloves, the Photoshop, and the rubber band slingshot. You're going to hurt somebody. Most likely yourself. Go back to the "Freshman" pranks and start again. Or just give up and take up knitting. It's safer for everyone!

Hellshire University Transcript
Office of the Registrar

Name: Creepy and Antisocial
Graduate of the Class of People Who Deserve to Die
Major: Psychology   **Minor:** Wartime Studies and Dance

Freshman Year—1st Semester

Intro to Psychology	A
Intro to Counterculture	A
Intro to World History	A
Intro to Women's Studies	D+

Freshman Year—2nd Semester

Psychology 150: Mind Control and Mental Torture	A
Music Department: Heavy Metal in the New Millennium	A
Intro to Modern Dance	C
History: Ancient Warfare	A

Sophomore Year—1st Semester

Psychology 280: Adolescent Psych	A
History: Modern Dance	D
History: Medieval Warfare	A
ROTC	

Sophomore Year—2nd Semester

Psychology 290: Great Historical Massacres and the Thinking Behind Them	A
Women's Psychology: How to Get a Date with One and Why	F
History: Modern Warfare	A
Photography: Shooting the Subject	Incomplete

(Comment: Class was never completed. Student misunderstood the topic.)
ROTC

Junior Year—1st Semester

Psychology 666: The Mind of the Serial Killer	A
Psychology 667: Anger and Children of Divorce	A-
History: General Warfare	A
Engineering Dept: Weapon Design and Function	A+

(by special request student was admitted without intro courses.)

ROTC

Junior Year—2nd Semester

Psychology 1220: Drugs and Behavior	B
Physical Fitness 101	A
Art Department: Figure Drawing	D-

(Restraining order obtained by model. Student forced to complete class from his dorm room.)

History: Great Political Battles	Incomplete

(Student failed to complete course claiming to have only read the word "battle" in the course list.)

ROTC

Senior Year—1st Semester

Independent Studies: Columbine and Its Aftermath	A
Physical Fitness 102	A
Girl's Books	B

(This grade was a plea bargain reached by the professor in order to keep the rest of her class from dropping the course. Student was asked never to return in exchange.)

Psychology 2000: Why Good People Go Bad	A

ROTC

Senior Year—2nd Semester

Note: *Student has not returned at date of issue. No one has seen the student in several weeks other than a few claims that a student of similar appearance has been seen skulking around outside the women's locker room. Family contacted. Didn't seem to know who he was.*

Diploma on hold.

Hellshire University Transcript
Office of the Registrar

Name: Will Do Anything to Get Some
Graduate of the Class of Lady Lovin'
Major: Women's Studies   **Minor:** Choir

Freshman Year—1st Semester

Intro to Women's Studies	C+
(Comments: Student distracted but his attendance was perfect.)	
Intro to Modern Dance	C
Choir I	C-
Intro to Psychology	B+

Freshman Year—2nd Semester

Intro to Biology	C
Psychology 122: Celebrity Psychology	B
Choir II	C-
History 112: *Her*Story	B-

Sophomore Year—1st Semester

English 101: Feminist Poetry	D-
(Comments: Great attendance and punctuality but attention plummeted as the weather warmed and students required fewer articles of clothing.)	
Performance Ensemble	C+
Feminine Sociology: Puppies, Rainbows, and Horses	A-
Fashion Buying 101	C

Sophomore Year—2nd Semester

The Music of Andrew Lloyd Webber	D
The Complete Works of Jane Austen	D
Biology 16: Female Physiology	A
Life Drawing	Incomplete
(Student failed to complete course work when he learned that the model's name was "Bruce.")	

Junior Year—1st Semester

Cleopatra to Pamela Lee: Women in History	A
French 101	A+
Great Broadway Performance	D
Sociology 69: The Women of Sex and the City	A

Junior Year—2nd Semester

Life Drawing — Incomplete

(Student did not complete the course after meeting the model, Big Bertha.)

French 202 — A+

(Comment: Student is a real pleasure to work with.—Professor Buttons Unbuttoned)

Choir III — D

Biology 16: Female Physiology — A+

(Comment: Student repeated course upon relating great interest in topic.)

Senior Year—1st Semester

Judy Blume: A Retrospective — C

French 303 — A+

History of Love — F

Life Drawing — Incomplete

(Comment: Course cancelled when model saw student and said there was no way in Hellshire that she would take her clothes off in front of that asshole!)

Senior Year—2nd Semester

Choir IV — A

(This grade was for showing up at the recital in spite of "the incident" with a few women in the class.)

Life Drawing — A+

(Comment: Course completed thanks to twin models named Svetlana and Masha.)

Biology 16: Female Physiology — A+

(Extra credit for teaching one of the lessons)

French 404 — F

(New teacher replaced Prof. Buttons Unbuttoned, named Mr. Dumas.)

Diploma Received.

About the Prankster

Mae B. Expelled was the kind of student who always raised her hand when the teacher asked for someone to clap the erasers. This mostly accomplished her goal of getting them to give her slightly better grades than she actually deserved. Whilst clapping said erasers she would often see if any of the chalk dust could be directed into the face of her arch nemesis, Urna Bette Tergrade, at recess.

In high school, Expelled used Voodoo, Wicca, and other religious practices that involved costumes in order to curse people she thought were either stupid, annoying, or flat-out evil. Not seeing the desired results, by college she graduated to the art of the prank. After the seventh university that had never heard of her finally let her graduate with a degree in Poly Sci, Expelled became a shut-in with a very precocious dog, Poo Per, who regularly left his business in the neighbor's yard. Now that she is old and gray, she likes to reminisce about the time she superglued the homecoming Queen's compact mirror to her face and the hamster she put in the dining hall coleslaw, but she no longer actually performs any pranks. She isn't allowed, what with being on probation in her home state and warrants pending in six others. But some day, when you least expect it. . . .

About the Accomplice

Joselin Linder, a writer and filmmaker, worked with Gigantic Pictures, an independent film studio in New York City, before coauthoring *The Good Girl's Guide to Living in Sin* (Adams Media), a book of advice on how to maintain a successful cohabitation. Her second book, *The Purity Test: Your Filth and Depravity Cheerfully Exposed by 2,000 Nosey Questions* (St. Martin's), taught her that if she could handle 2,000 dirty questions, there wasn't a whole lot she couldn't handle. Her next book, *The Good Girl's Guide to Getting It On* (Adams Media), offers advice from women about how to keep long-term relationships spicy. Cowritten with Elena Donovan Mauer, the book is slated for release in the winter of 2010. Linder is a founding member of the Stoned Crow Writers Workshop, a fiction group that has carried on a weekly meeting since 2005. Her popular blog on cohabitation can be found at *www.thegoodgirlsguidetolivinginsin .com*.

Linder currently lives and writes and Brooklyn. She and her boyfriend Aaron share a great apartment and their fantastic dog, Dee Dee Ramone. She learned while writing this book that Aaron's is a past rife with eggings.